Illustrations by **Phil Juliano**

Illustrations by **Taras Kharechko**

Cover by **Benedick Duria**

D0611094

Disclaimer

Thanks for choosing to purchase this activity book!

If you enjoy it, we would be very grateful if you posted a short review on Amazon! Your support does make a difference and we read every review.

If you would like to leave a review, just head on over to this book's Amazon page and click "Write a customer review".

Thank you for your support!

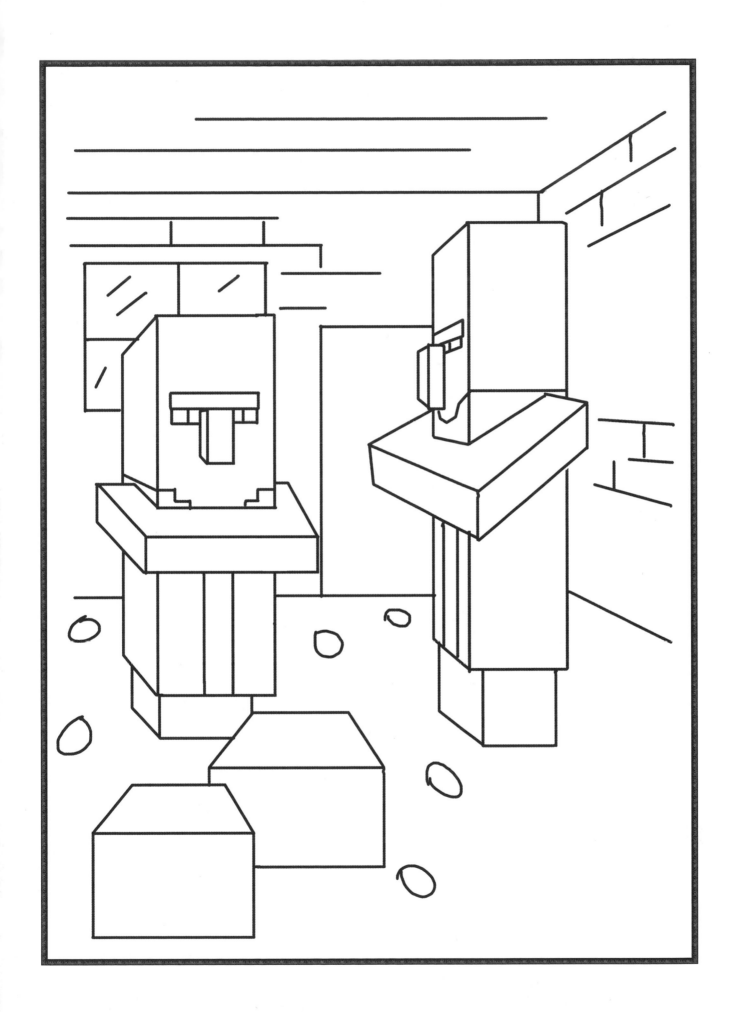

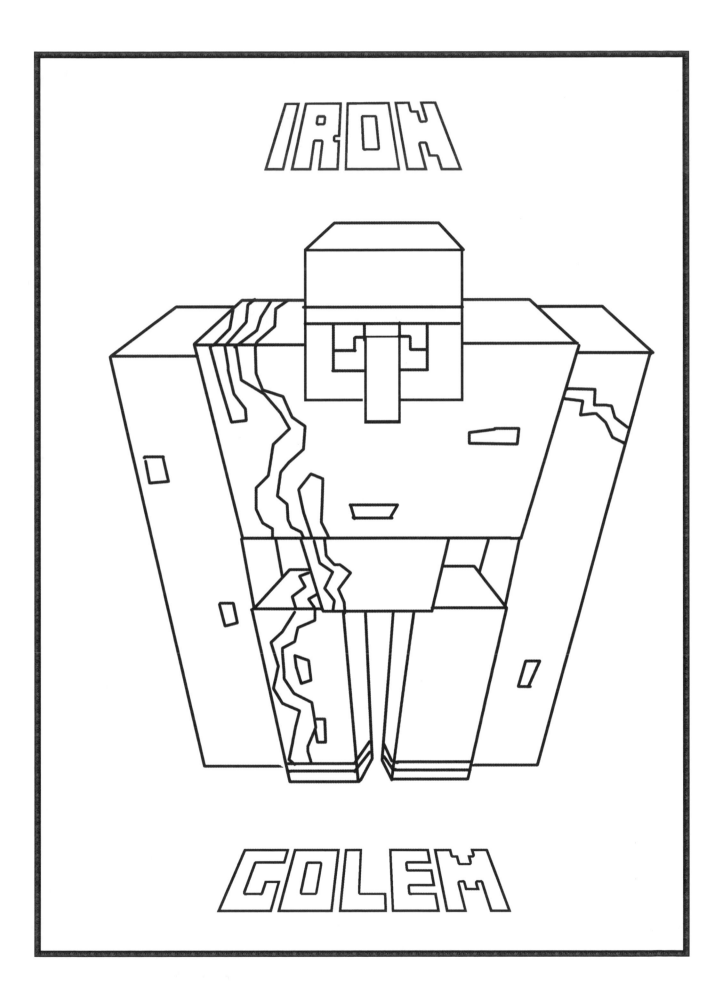

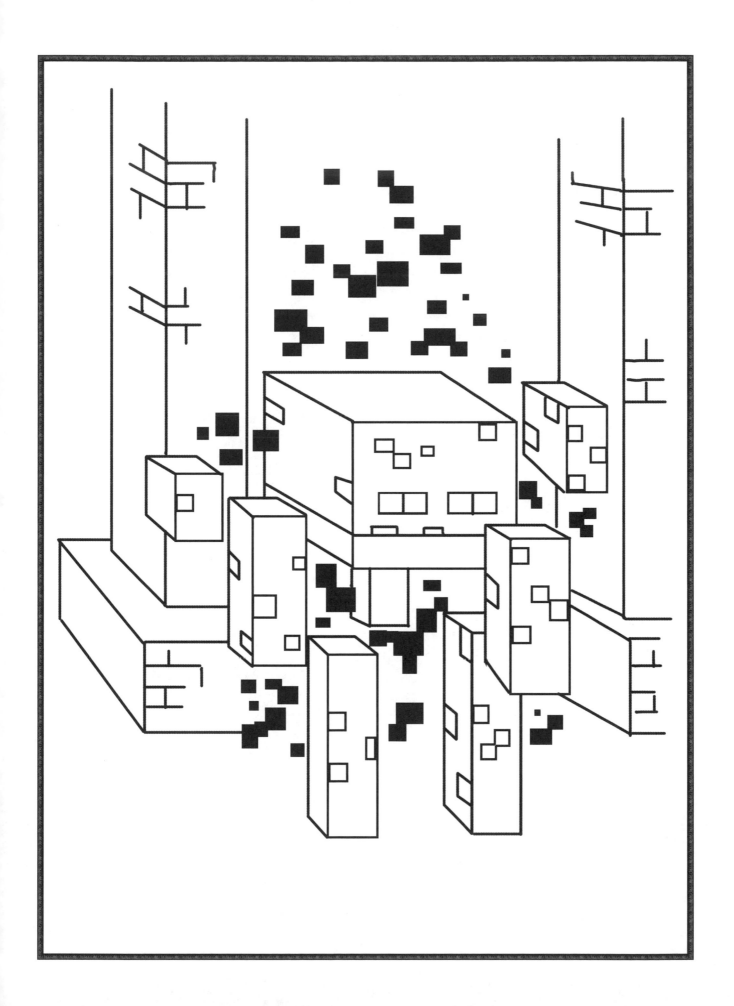

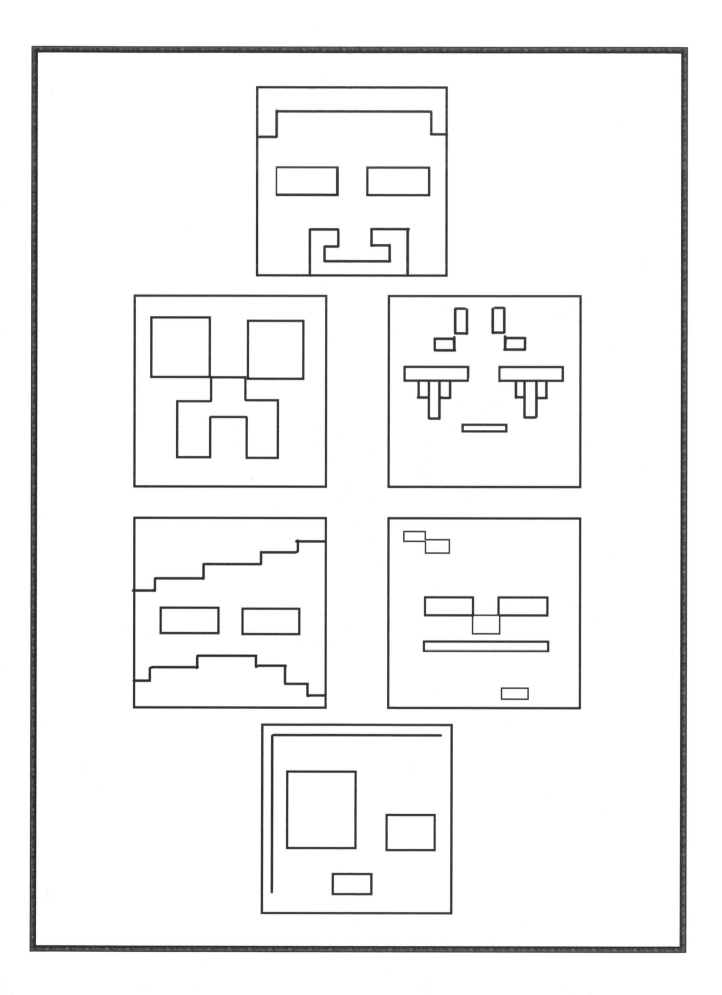

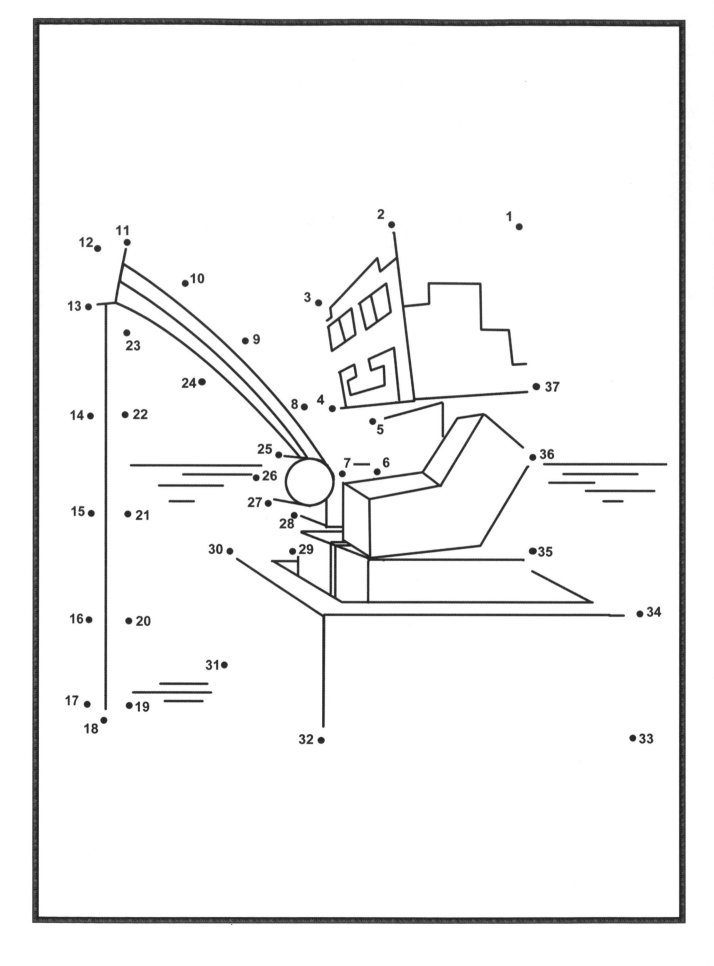

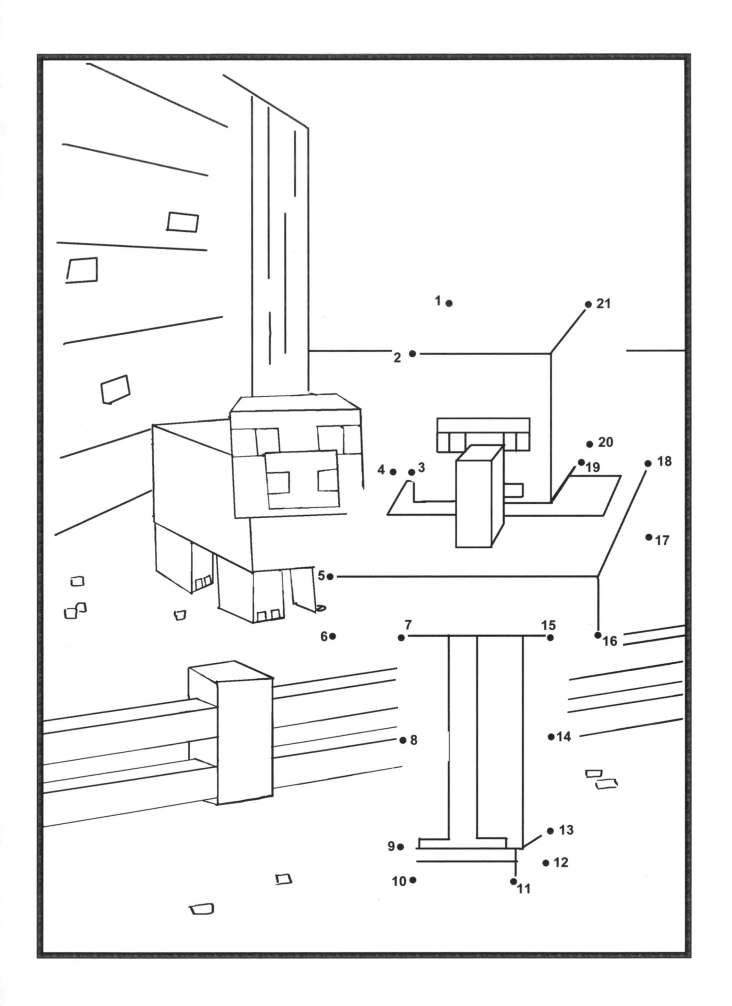

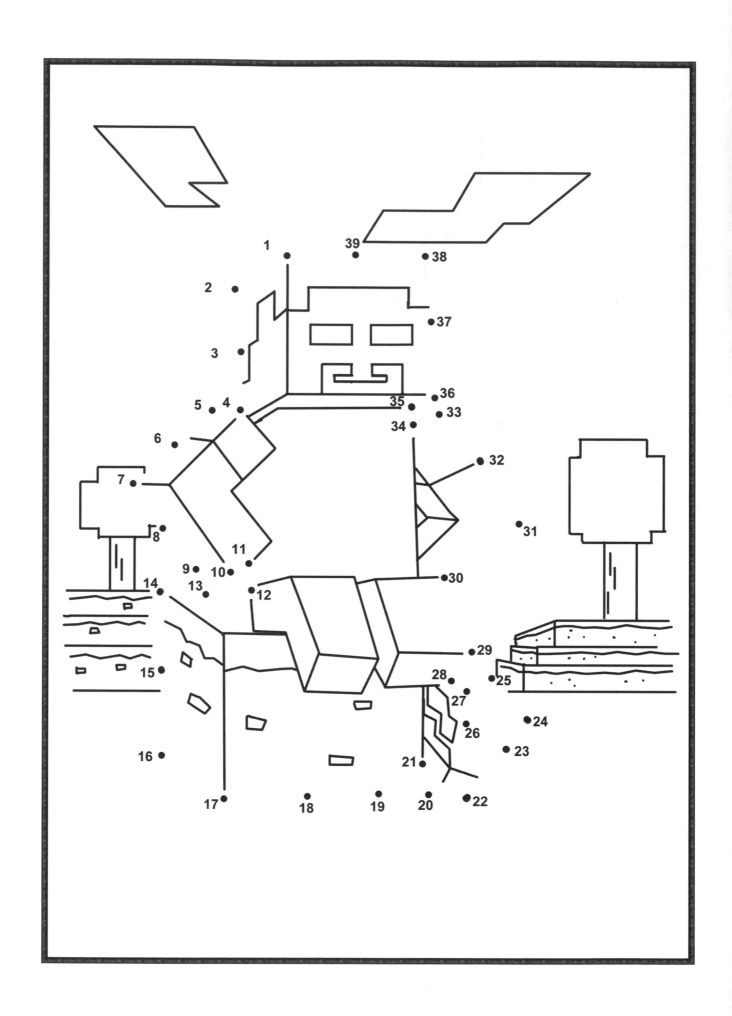

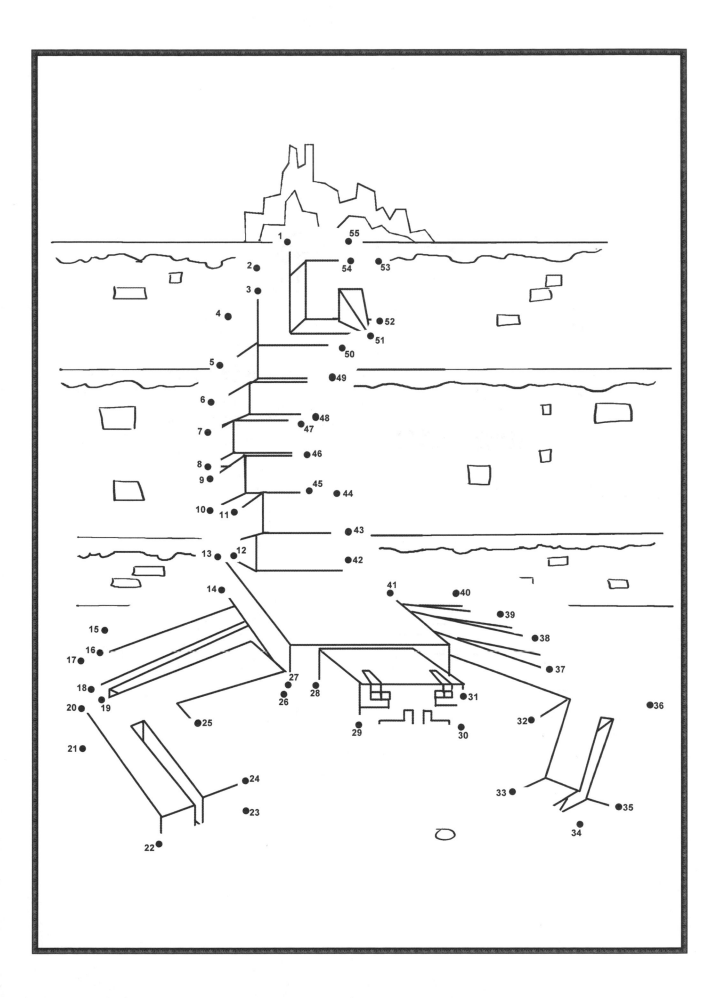

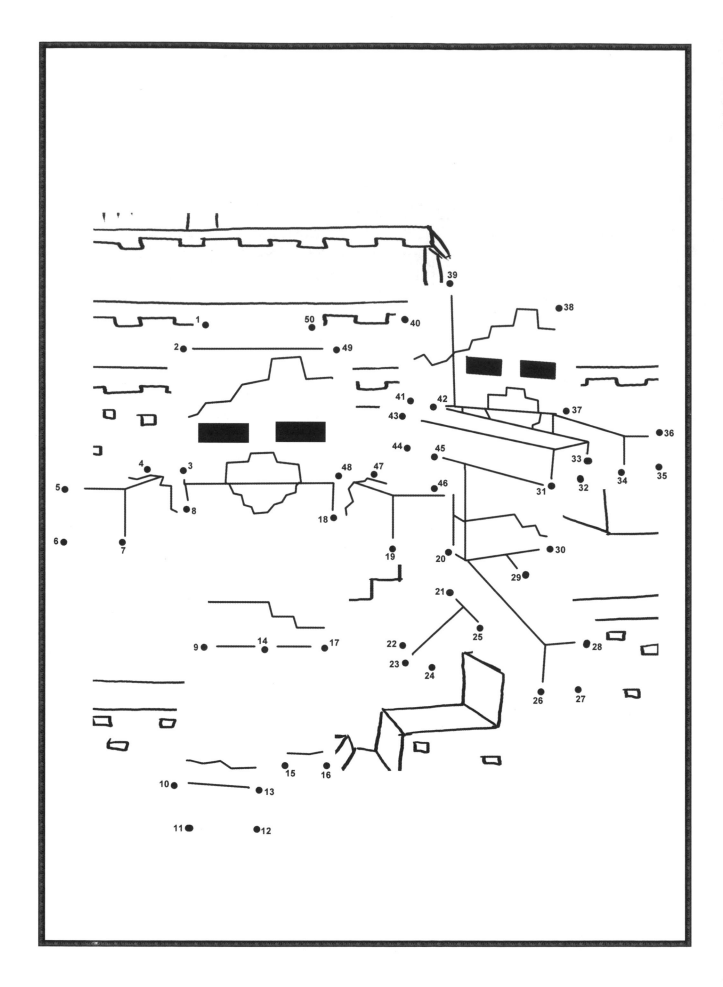

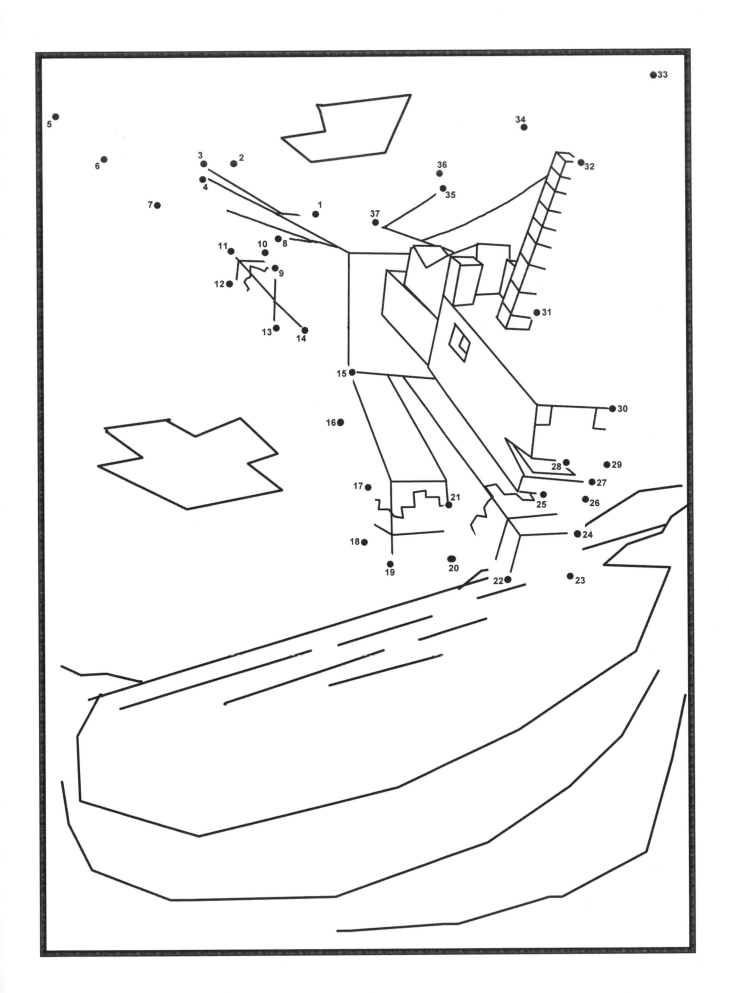

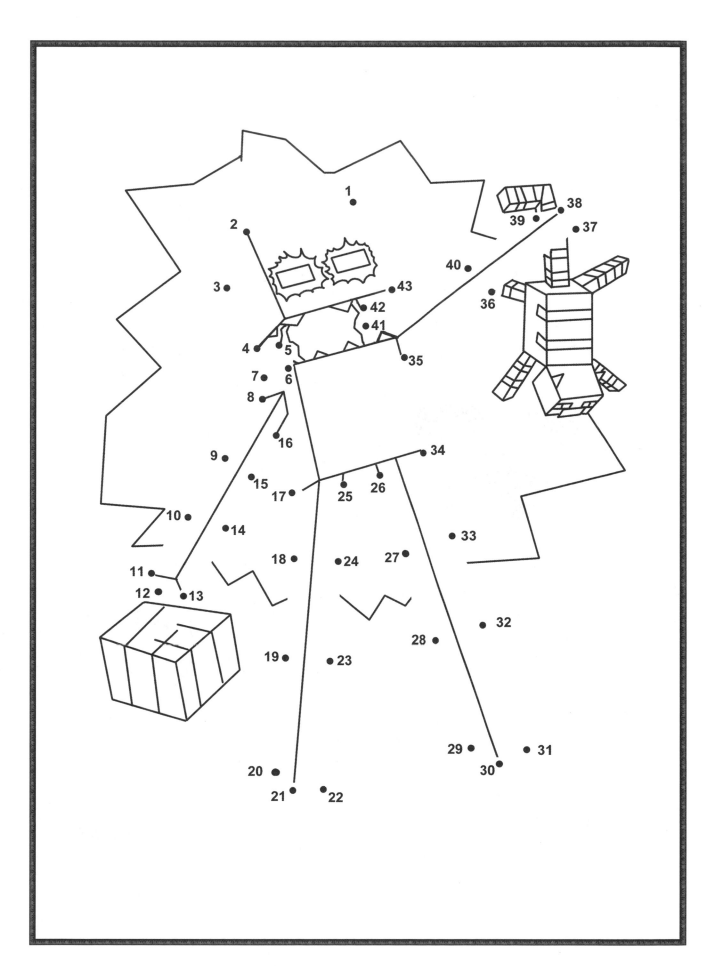

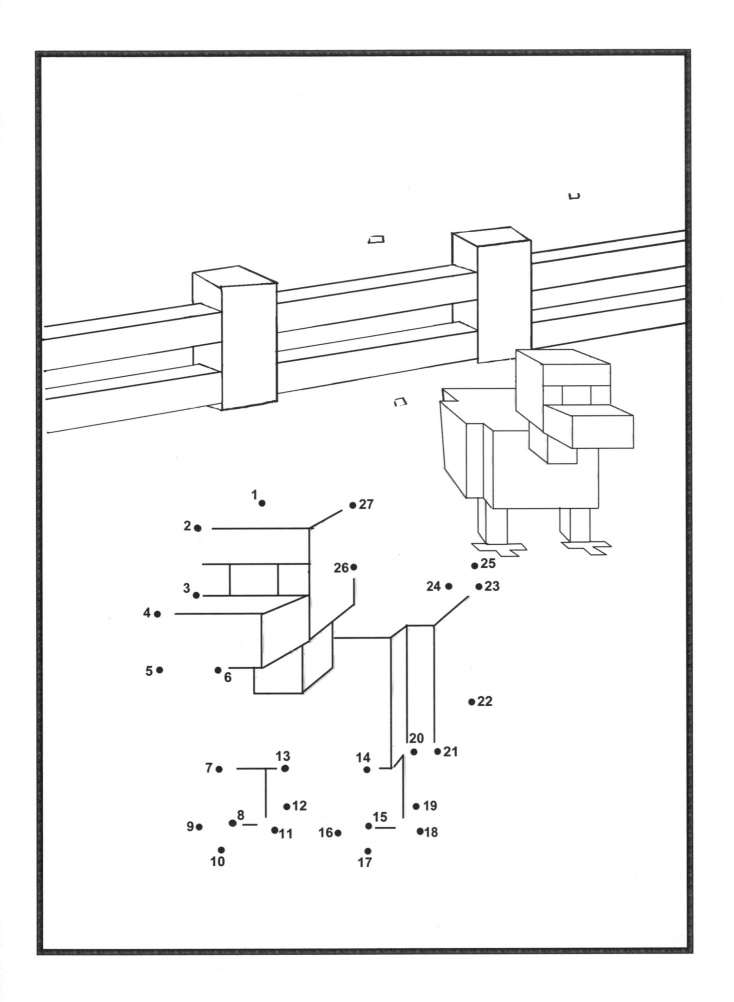

HELP STEVE FIND HIS PICKAXE!

Start

Finish

 # HELP STEVE FIND HIS SWORD!

HELP THE UNICORN FIND HER APPLE!

SPOT THE DIFFERENCE!

There are seven things different in these two pictures...can you find them?

SPOT THE DIFFERENCE...IN THE DESERT!

There five things different in these two pictures...can you find them?

SPOT THE DIFFERENCE...IN THE PLAINS!

There five things different in these two pictures...can you find them?

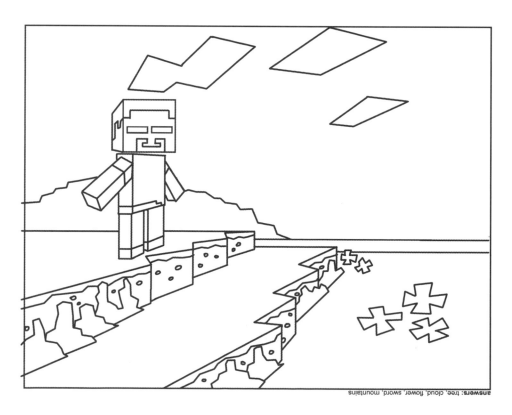

SPOT THE DIFFERENCE...IN THE VILLAGE!

There five things different in these two pictures...can you find them?

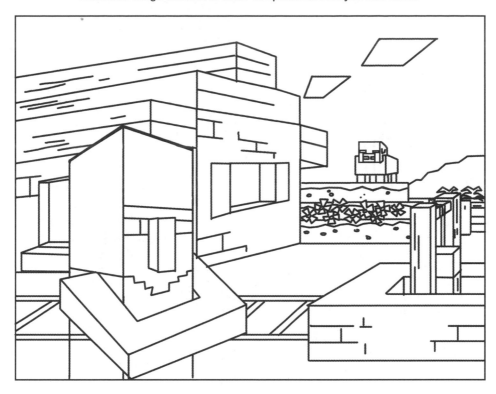

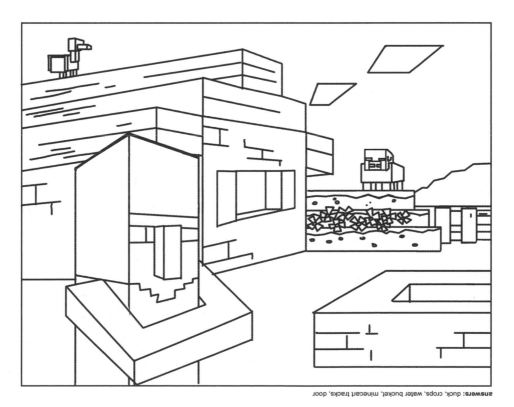

SPOT THE DIFFERENCE...IN THE TAIGA!

There are seven things different in these two pictures...can you find them?

EASY CROSSWORD!

Across
6. TNT
7. material
8. dead enemy with rotten flesh
Down
1. demon
2. nugget
3. black enemy that can teleport
4. animal that provides beef and leather
5. creature that blows up

YUM! FOODS IN MINECRAFT

Across
4. sweet treat but not very filling
7. makes cakes and cookies
8. only found in chests down mineshafts
9. cooked clucker
10. water and a rod catches these
Down
1. oinkers provide this food
2. three pieces of wheat make this
3. edible but poisonous
5. found in locked dungeons boxes
6. dropped by passive cluckers
7. cooked cow

AREAS OF THE MINECRAFT WORLD

Across
3. very mountainous area
6. sandy areas on shores of oceans
7. area with sand dunes and cacti
9. wet area with witch huts
Down
1. plains large flat area with lots of snow
2. regions found in Minecraft world
4. place where Endermen are spawned
5. hill with flat top
8. area filled with spruce and fern
10. flat area with rolling hills and grass

TOOLS AND WEAPONS

Across
1. long range weapon
4. used as flint and steel or ammo
5. large sharp weapon
6. used to mine stone
7. long range ammunition
8. allows you to ride animals
9. breaks wooden blocks
10. used to set things on fire
Down
1. transports lava, water and milk
2. shaves sheep
3. tills grass and dirt
4. used to catch fish
8. breaks sand and dirt

MINECRAFT ANIMALS

ACROSS

6 Hops around aimlessly and like carrots and dandelions
7 Water creature with eight arms
8 With saddles are the fastest transport
9 Poisonous neutral mob
11 Creepers don't like them
12 Tameable friend that teleports back to player

DOWN

1 Result of lightning and pork providing animal
2 Flying cave creature
3 Variation of Overworld herd animal
4 Pork provider
5 Egg laying passive mob
7 Wool and mutton provider
10 Herd animal of the Overworld

CHARACTERS WORD SEARCH

```
S I G R G R U C O E P A F G M
P L X A E Y C A J I H F O E G
R T I H T S A H G B R V W R O
C E C M E F R F H M S A D J L
V R P F E C C E B O F B H H E
A M O E B D R C J Z J T K D M
K X J L E O I U V N L C N E O
R D A C B R O U W G K G O E V
X Z H R D W C S T E V E D N X
E J I N Z Q X A P Z P Z Q L Y
Y N C D S F Q O M Z I U D M Y
E V O Q J I A R I K E H J U W
N A M R E D N E W Y H V Y C H
X Y W U D J N L P W O A C W G
A G I I M V T Y I J I X M X R
```

ARCHER
BLAZE
CREEPER
ENDERMAN
GHAST
GOLEM
HEROBRINE
SLIME
STEVE
ZOMBIE

ITEMS WORD SEARCH

```
I O U B J E C T A I J G L W B
U T O E D O R Z Q T U O E O K
T O P A M A E V Q L H L A R Y
K N P P C D I A M O N D T R O
W S A E S W O R D R O U H A N
W S N G Z Q U U Q E O W E K E
S I Y F T F E E B X S D R T A
M E L W E G B S M A M I S D C
T L J Q V A N J A N D U L S J
T O U J C A T Q S A X K E H I
X A G A I U Y H U M D Q P O T
M J O N R B R R E E Z A L B K
I A L B I X Q U E R T F Y I P
W O Z I V O S I R Q R C T N B
C M I T U I K E Z Q C L K B D
```

ARROW
AXE
BEEF
BLAZE
BOAT
BOOK
COMPASS
DIAMOND
FEATHER
GOLD
INGOT
LEATHER
MINECART
RODS
SPADE
SWORD

PLACES WORD SEARCH

```
T I K E M F D R N R T U H V R W F S D R
I F S E O S E E I R E E H B N D Y P S R
V N A R P Q S E A G R H R N H S C T B P
J I E H Z L E N T H R Y T F V H A H W F
L S L Z S I R O N C O C Y E A C V D A C
T B S L E E T U U R Y U K N N T E R I D
N O Z S A N N G O Z S Q S P Z I M Q L K
C M N W N G U I M Z O M B E B W P E T P
P X J H K F E L M J H O T N S S I C D F
M G S T G Y T L A J R N M M F F L I D T
N C Y H N W R F O M W V L Y O S Z A N M
U E E L G N U J L Y G R N D Q A K A O N
D G V H P B E N F Z P R O R M B L K P K
U J W F M A O W O T U C K T F V P N F B
M E R Y J E B H D X T T N R Q V N I E D
A P H A G A Z A J N F K E O C E A N I I
Q A L N X I A P L I S W A N L X L Z B A
F K U R V F Q R W D S C W S X H Q S A O
Y D O I L D V E W B M G Y M U X M N Y X
J L S H E L T E R S G S Q L F O Z E A N
```

CAVE
DESERT
DUNGEON
FARM
FIELD
FOREST
HOUSE
HUT
JUNGLE
MINESHAFT
MOUNTAIN
NETHER
OCEAN
SHELTER
VILLAGE
WITCHS

MYTHS AND MONSTERS WORD SEARCH

```
Z V L G H M B H A K Z B P G F G R I I K Z I O F L L A N S L
C O C C T Q Q U F J D K L N N A O M A N I T Q D W Z V A U K
C T L P O R D N L I J X B P J P L M C U X A Z V A P U W Z Z
N E D L O G Q T B F H S X T R V B A B C A Y F M T F C Y X J
E C N B S V K E M M S I E H R T N W T H K T R G W P T R K J
N Y C Q W N P R S E G R D J U J N B I D I N M D V L M M X L
G M Z E K G F S K I Z X Y C O M H X X K B I O Z X C P B K B
W F I I F X F V G J E X F B V K B B M Q X C W C R N U B X Q
C M B I Z G R H I L L V O R H U O C A T I Y Z N G W O D Z F
X W N U E P Z Q I K Z K R J F U P P A F E Q O Q R A D B P D
L Q P D P R E O B J Z Q W F A F E E M Y C S M J N L J T Q O
W T F F Z O O D S F J R G D D B K A N S F Y I Z S O F F I V
H W D R K W J G Y O O M E Z K N B I J S M H G B V G R L Q Y
S X X K R H E N Z N E A J H K M D W M Z P Z O R E U M T I K
R E G N I T R E P L O W M A D A J I R G H T Z B A C G C D A
H S C V X X R Z O B F U D C H U H N R U E N X T U Q H Q S O
L H O E Z V T G P R I A R C V C R A I E G E O M Z J O F C H
W W G Q P R I Q N L X J I G Q L R W L J C N I H M Z Y H L B
L G X D E O P O C T U O N R F F A I V S I D T T W C I J P V
X A S V G H L E O U S A D B I I F Q O M D I E Y N M J L G Y
X O W P Z U J A S W P R T C D E T W A U O O F Y E A J E P G
B F G D C L Y D K G S F I Y A C S L M Z W R O R I K I C Q X
F A U Q Q F J A M C M C O B X L B D E K F D A V X E F G C L
V R U L L F M A W H A S B Y O L J U A D Q N H W R D R Y V Q
H F C S U U R I L M E J A F W S F O U R N E J V Z N X A K R
Q S Z H S V E R F H A L A R V A A Z Q H U D B L I T S U N E
B G N C U P T Y E F O X O K A X C N A M T C I P C A H P K D
Y E J N T G B R Q V U G Z Y G E Q V D Q Y Q Z L E M S X A F
C C P H E V N T Q D N H U B Y L B D M K I H A C U U Z V I G
S O K G C J A A O E V K K W X R D I G E R Y Z P M W A T J O
```

AQUA	GOLEM
BEAR	HILL
BLITSUNE	HUNTERS
CETUS	JACKALOPE
CHIMERA	MAN
CLAY	MINOTAUR
DENDROID	RAM
DROP	SAND
FAIRIES	WOLPERTINGER
GIANT	WYRM
GOLDEN	

ANIMALS WORD SEARCH

```
M O O S H R O O M K F N E U Y I X I L V M M I H H C U H L M
J N Z I C R O F P L F D F X T I P A P J W O N R L J Z M X E
B Y Q U D O J Q O D B V A D C Z A A G J L G W A R L T E Q E
Z M W C R L R W C G R L S A V M F A Q C L B N C U R S U J Z
Y T T D W A A P J C Z U R W T K H Y F B G J J C R C N O W B
C X V O N C U A I U N I C Q Y F E O C H R B A O R A K L H V
Z V B W E N N B T O B L E E S V D G X J M S L O J T S H C L
U L P A I V E D P A N D S U Y C C C V N Z K K N M C E W W Z
T Y R C R P N Q Y L E G M A I T N J D R Q N J I Y A T U H E
A Z O W E F E C O D L P F V T S C U Z U U C I I E T T Y V G
N R Y E J V J I E Y P Z I N E T U D N L X L B F N S O F T V
N V W Q T Q E T D K U F F M I N T Z Y O D M O U D N H I L C
H K G W U R K U R T P R V Q D Z R L C X N X E J E J U M F O
Z S J W E B C T A R Y B I L F W P X J H V T J O R K K Q O E
V G B D X J U U P L C C B H W C J U K K U S K P Y H T M U T
R Y I T U Y D K O F K I X B Z L D P Q U H T U Z E H Z D R S
X P Y R Y X I T E M I Y K Z M R T R T I X I U P D K E O B N
S I X E A Z J X L U Q S I Q E J T I J A B U X Y G S Y J I O
Q D S O F H K R N Z V E F Q T S N A A W N E P M Z A R T C H
B Y K S V F Y B H X N C A K H J T T P I J N V J D X Z E H D
J J D O N R A X J U Y K L L Q K G T Q U J X Z M Y E J B P P
H B L P Y G L R C F N Z U P I S M B J O E K L F T J R M M W
S I E J G O U A I H L K S X V T L M X I S H F M A D P Y D K
D H E V H G W T G G Y C I E T L C J S B W I Z W Y C F F E V
F Y G O A B Z G N W Y I N K H X E N T C E C O P N P Z N A G
R S R R T C D A H U P D R A G O N A S G J C J X H T I F I N
R S S D I Y G Q U X M E X N T W K M Z H L F T K K X I G Y I
E T J P P O C A J D Y U M X P G B O R E E B C O W I J M E D
P B A I D B J M G I A J J C O I C B K Z Q E G M W C Y O P J
S U P O T C O Z H G D W J V B C W F M I X D P A L A O K Z J
```

CAT	LEOPARD
CAVE	MOOSHROOM
COW	OCTOPUS
DRAGON	PIG
DUCK	RACCOON
ENDER	SCORPION
FOX	SHEEP
GIRAFFE	SPIDER
HORSE	UNICORN
KOALA	WOLF

DNERRBINEE

_____

EEERCPR

_____

IDADNMO

_____

ALRBEDZSO

_____

WUORNDPGE

_____

RNDOGERDNEA

_____

IKPECAX

_____

DSROW

_____

INMARECT

_____

IEFTSITEATC

_____

MINECRAFT WORD SCRAMBLE!

Unscramble all the words to uncover the different items found in Minecraft!

STGELOOWN

_____

OBIEIZ ENMMGP

_____

SATGH

_____

ROLTHN TEAERP

_____

OROSMHMU

_____

SOANBIID

_____

RCDOEKB

_____

BCMUM GEAA

_____

ONSLETEK

_____

EAZBL

_____

IN THE NETHER!

Unscramble all the words to uncover the different items found in The Nether!

MINECRAFT ANIMAL PARTS MATCH-UP

Parts are parts, right? Draw a line between the animal and its parts!

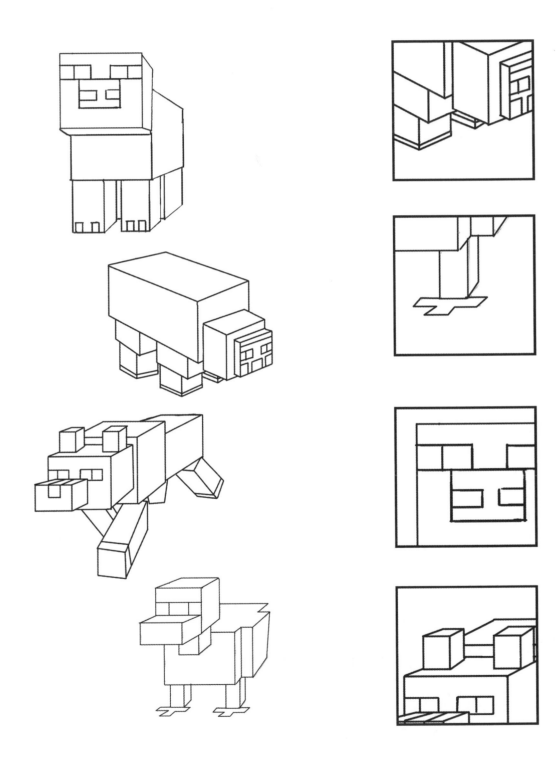

ITEMS MATCHING GAME

Draw a line from the names in the middle to the
matching items on each side

bed

enchanted book

hoe

potion

pickaxe

melon

sword

record

leather

hatchet

map

brick

bow

blaze powder

CREATURE MATCH!

Draw a line from the creature on
the left to their name on the right!
Ready, set...go!

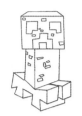

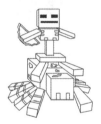

GHAST

CREEPER

ENDERMAN

ZOMBIE

**SKELETON
ARCHER**

HEROBRINE

COUNT 'EM AND MATCH 'EM!

Count the number of items in each box and match
them with the correct number

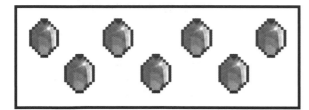

7

10

2

3

5

MINECRAFT SYLLABLE MATCH

Draw a line from the syllable on the left
to the syllable right to make Minecraft words!

Cree	bie	➡ _____
Ender	brine	➡ _____
Zom	axe	➡ _____
Hero	rod	➡ _____
Moosh	ow	➡ _____
pick	room	➡ _____
fishing	per	➡ _____
arr	man	➡ _____

WHAT DO THEY DO?

Draw a line from the description on the
left to the item on the right!

mines stones and
blocks faster
                                    blaze rods

used as ammunition
for bows and can harm
characters from a distance
                                    axe

breaks wooden
blocks faster
                                    diamond

used to set things
on fire and light TNT
and Nether portals
                                    pickaxe

used to create blaze
powder and brewing
stands
                                    flint and steel

rare ore used to create
the best weapons, tools
and armor
                                    arrows

WHO'S SHADOW IS IT?

Match each creature to its shadow!

SNOW GOLEM

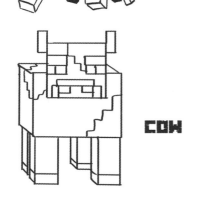

OCTOPUS

COW

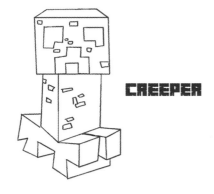

CREEPER

1+5	9-8	4x4	16-3	5x3	19-2	9x2	1+5	9-8	4x4	16-3	5x3	19-2	9x2
16-3	5x3	19-2	9x2	32x2	50+12	79-6	30x2	50+6	6x9	9x2	46-29	23-7	16-3
9x2	46-29	70x10	9x8	14x10	139+2	20x7	25x5	14x10	139+1	25+27	20x3	9-8	4x4
23-7	79x1	12x10	76+9	89+30	76+9	29x5	16x10	99-6	22x4	20x7	29x5	50+12	46-29
9x2	30x2	78+2	94-7	16x10	25x6	99-6	160x1	29x5	94-7	76+9	70x10	9x8	17-3
16-3	50+6	23+7	32x2	50+12	29x5	120-1	50x2	29x3	32x2	50+12	23+7	32x2	4x4
4x4	6x9	8x4	29-8	46-9	79x1	32x2	50+12	79-6	160x1	12x10	2x22	70x10	9-8
46-29	25+27	7+22	5x5	20x2	99-6	8x4	29-8	46-9	22x4	7+22	8x6	50+12	5x3
1+5	20x3	29-8	46-9	16-3	7+36	23+7	5x5	20x2	89+30	30x2	7+36	78+2	46-29
16-3	17-3	2x22	7+22	4x4	46-29	8x4	46-9	20x2	29-8	50+6	9x8	16-3	17-3
9x2	4x4	8x6	8x4	29-8	1+5	7+22	9x3	8x4	120-1	6x9	32x2	9x2	4x4
23-7	46-29	7+36	7+22	5x5	20x2	29-8	34-7	7+22	29-8	25+27	70x10	23-7	46-29
9x2	1+5	16-3	50+6	4x6	23+7	9x3	8x4	29-8	46-9	50+12	17-3	9x2	1+5
16-3	19-2	9x2	25+27	20x3	30+2	34-7	7+22	5x5	20x2	78+2	4x4	16-3	19-2
4x4	23-7	23-7	46-29	32x2	50+12	79-6	70x10	9x8	79x1	19-2	46-29	4x4	23-7
46-29	9-8	9x2	1+5	23-7	9-8	4x4	16-3	5x3	19-2	9x2	1+5	46-29	9-8

1-20 White

21-40 Light grey

41-60 Grey

61-80 Dark grey

81-100 Orange

101-120 Pink

121-140 Light orange

141-160 Yellow

Color key:

- 1-20 White
- 21-40 Green
- 41-60 Blue
- 61-80 Light brown
- 81-100 Brown
- 101-120 Dark brown
- 121-140 Pink
- 141-160 Navy
- 161-180 Violet

Each grid cell shows an expression over a result (written as `expr / value`).

12x/3	20x/2	15x/2	13+/23	61-/24	12x/3	12x/3	20x/6	15x/10	99+/8	160-/44	59x/2	20x/6	15x/8	99+/13	12x/3	20x/2	15x/2	13+/23	61-/24	12x/3
35+/4	4x/9	15+/22	61-/30	20+/17	35+/4	95+/6	4x/30	15+/102	131-/30	86+/27	75+/44	4x/30	15+/102	131-/30	35+/4	4x/9	15+/22	61-/30	20+/17	35+/4
17x/3	19x/2	18+/12	8+/32	61-/30	17x/3	17x/6	59x/2	18+/101	8+/97	141-/30	58x/30	59x/2	18+/101	8+/97	17x/3	19x/2	18+/12	8+/32	61-/30	17x/3
45-/12	40x/1	21+/9	51-/11	20+/19	45-/12	15+/102	10+/67	45+/32	85-/11	12x/6	90-/17	60+/9	41+/39	86+/27	45-/12	40x/1	21+/9	51-/11	20+/19	45-/12
6x/6	39x/1	20+/13	78-/41	61-/24	6x/6	42x/16	90-/22	31+/42	19x/4	32+/37	55+/22	40+/37	95-/12	65+/17	6x/6	39x/1	20+/13	78-/41	61-/24	6x/6
12x/3	20x/2	15x/2	13+/23	61-/24	12x/3	10+/67	61-/42	19x/9	95-/31	21+/39	41+/39	3x/60	21-/9	90-/17	12x/3	20x/2	15x/2	13+/23	61-/24	12x/3
35+/4	4x/9	15+/22	61-/30	20+/17	35+/4	90-/22	31+/42	19x/4	85-/4	12x/7	90-/7	19x/4	90-/22	31+/42	35+/4	4x/9	15+/22	61-/30	20+/17	35+/4
17x/3	19x/2	18+/12	8+/32	61-/30	17x/3	60+/9	41+/39	91-/13	25x/4	32+/60	74+/22	91-/13	60+/9	41+/39	17x/3	19x/2	18+/12	8+/32	61-/30	17x/3
45-/12	40x/1	21+/9	51-/11	20+/19	45-/12	40+/37	65+/12	12x/10	35x/4	99+/37	55+/81	20x/6	40+/37	65+/12	45-/12	40x/1	21+/9	51-/11	20+/19	45-/12
6x/6	39x/1	20+/13	78-/41	61-/24	6x/6	42x/16	90-/47	20x/6	15x/8	99+/13	160-/44	59x/2	42x/16	90-/47	6x/6	39x/1	20+/13	78-/41	61-/24	6x/6
20x/2	30+/17	42+/6	90-/47	31+/22	20x/3	30+/17	45+/12	40+/37	65+/12	95-/31	39x/2	80-/7	30+/17	42+/6	90-/47	31+/22	20x/3	30+/17	45+/12	12x/3
4x/9	55-/11	3x/16	50+/9	21+/39	15x/3	78+/32	30+/17	90-/47	21+/39	61-/15	15x/12	55-/11	3x/16	50+/9	21+/39	61-/15	15x/3	78+/32	35+/4	
19x/2	61-/15	20x/3	30+/17	45+/12	55-/11	42+/16	90-/47	21+/39	61-/15	15x/3	15x/3	78+/32	61-/15	20x/3	30+/17	45+/12	55-/11	42+/16	90-/47	17x/3
40x/1	30+/17	45+/12	42+/6	90-/47	21+/39	61-/15	55-/11	45+/12	55-/11	42x/16	21+/39	61-/15	30+/17	45+/12	42+/6	90-/47	21+/39	61-/15	55-/11	45-/12
39x/15	61-/17	20x/3	30+/17	45+/12	55-/11	42+/16	90-/47	21+/39	61-/15	15x/3	15x/3	78+/32	61-/15	20x/3	30+/17	45+/12	55-/11	42+/16	90-/47	6x/6
20x/2	90-/22	31+/42	19x/4	32+/37	55+/22	61-/15	55-/11	45+/12	55-/11	42+/6	21+/39	61-/15	30+/17	45+/12	90-/22	31+/42	19x/4	32+/37	55+/22	12x/3
4x/9	60+/39	41+/39	91-/13	15x/5	78+/1	42+/6	90-/47	21+/39	61-/15	15x/3	15x/3	78+/32	61-/15	20x/9	60+/39	41+/39	91-/13	15x/5	78+/1	39x/1
19x/2	40+/37	65+/12	95-/31	39x/2	80-/7	78+/32	61-/15	55-/11	3x/16	50+/9	21+/39	61-/15	15x/3	78+/32	40+/37	65+/12	95-/31	39x/2	80-/7	20x/2
40x/1	42x/16	90-/47	21+/39	61-/15	95-/17	61-/15	30+/17	20x/3	30+/17	45+/12	55-/11	42+/6	90-/47	42x/16	90-/47	21+/39	61-/15	95-/17	4x/9	
39x/1	10+/67	45+/32	85-/11	12x/6	90-/17	78+/32	61-/15	30+/17	45+/12	42+/6	90-/47	21+/39	61-/15	55-/11	10+/67	45+/32	85-/11	12x/6	90-/17	19x/2
19x/2	90-/22	31+/42	19x/4	32+/37	55+/22	61-/15	15x/3	15x/3	20x/3	30+/17	45+/12	90-/47	90-/22	31+/42	19x/4	32+/37	55+/22	40x/1		
40x/1	60+/39	41+/39	91-/13	15x/5	78+/1	42+/6	90-/47	21+/39	61-/15	15x/3	15x/3	78+/32	61-/15	20x/9	60+/39	41+/39	91-/13	15x/5	78+/1	39x/1
39x/1	40+/37	65+/12	95-/31	39x/2	80-/7	18x/10	31+/149	19x/9	3x/60	55+/111	18x/10	10x/16	55-/11	42+/6	40+/37	65+/12	95-/31	39x/2	80-/7	19x/2
20x/2	42x/16	90-/47	21+/39	61-/15	95-/17	60+/150	99+/79	191-/13	15x/11	78+/100	60+/150	32+/137	90-/57	61-/15	42x/16	90-/47	21+/39	61-/15	95-/17	40x/1
4x/9	10+/67	45+/32	85-/11	12x/6	90-/17	40+/125	65+/112	195-/21	89x/2	180-/7	40+/125	65+/112	195-/21	89x/2	10+/67	45+/32	85-/11	12x/6	90-/17	39x/1
12x/3	20x/2	15x/2	13+/23	61-/24	12x/3	42x/4	190-/17	21+/157	164-/3	195-/17	42x/4	190-/17	21+/157	195-/3	12x/3	20x/2	15x/2	13+/23	61-/24	12x/3
35+/4	4x/9	15+/22	61-/30	20+/17	35+/4	10+/167	45+/132	185-/11	30x/6	190-/17	10+/167	45+/132	185-/11	30x/6	35+/4	4x/9	15+/22	61-/30	20+/17	35+/4
17x/3	19x/2	18+/12	8+/32	61-/30	17x/3	1x/175	5+/158	20x/9	32+/137	55+/122	1x/175	5+/158	20x/9	32+/137	17x/3	19x/2	18+/12	8+/32	61-/30	17x/3
45-/12	40x/1	21+/9	51-/11	20+/19	45-/12	60+/119	41+/139	191-/13	15x/11	1+/178	60+/119	41+/139	191-/13	15x/11	45-/12	40x/1	21+/9	51-/11	20+/19	45-/12
6x/6	39x/1	20+/13	78-/41	61-/24	6x/6	42x/4	190-/17	21+/157	164-/3	195-/17	42x/4	190-/17	21+/157	164-/3	6x/6	39x/1	20+/13	78-/41	61-/24	6x/6
12x/3	20x/2	15x/2	13+/23	61-/24	12x/3	10+/167	45+/132	185-/11	30x/6	190-/17	10+/167	45+/132	185-/11	30x/6	12x/3	20x/2	15x/2	13+/23	61-/24	12x/3
35+/4	4x/9	15+/22	61-/30	20+/17	35+/4	1x/175	5+/158	20x/9	32+/137	55+/122	1x/175	5+/158	20x/9	32+/137	35+/4	4x/9	15+/22	61-/30	20+/17	35+/4
17x/3	19x/2	18+/12	8+/32	61-/30	17x/3	60+/119	41+/139	191-/13	15x/11	1+/178	60+/119	41+/139	191-/13	15x/11	17x/3	19x/2	18+/12	8+/32	61-/30	17x/3
45-/12	40x/1	21+/9	51-/11	20+/19	45-/12	20x/9	10x/16	90+/57	190-/17	21+/157	164-/3	99+/49	51x/9	42x/3	45-/12	40x/1	21+/9	51-/11	20+/19	45-/12
6x/6	39x/1	20+/13	78-/41	61-/24	6x/6	42x/4	190-/17	21+/157	164-/3	195-/17	42x/4	190-/17	21+/157	164-/3	6x/6	39x/1	20+/13	78-/41	61-/24	6x/6
12x/3	20x/2	15x/2	13+/23	61-/24	12x/3	10+/167	45+/132	185-/11	30x/6	190-/17	10+/167	45+/132	185-/11	30x/6	12x/3	20x/2	15x/2	13+/23	61-/24	12x/3
35+/4	4x/9	15+/22	61-/30	20+/17	35+/4	1x/175	5+/158	20x/9	32+/137	55+/122	1x/175	5+/158	20x/9	32+/137	35+/4	4x/9	15+/22	61-/30	20+/17	35+/4
17x/3	19x/2	18+/12	8+/32	61-/30	17x/3	60+/119	41+/139	191-/13	15x/11	1+/178	60+/119	41+/139	191-/13	15x/11	17x/3	19x/2	18+/12	8+/32	61-/30	17x/3
45-/12	40x/1	21+/9	51-/11	20+/19	45-/12	42x/4	190-/17	21+/157	164-/3	195-/17	42x/4	190-/17	21+/157	164-/3	45-/12	40x/1	21+/9	51-/11	20+/19	45-/12
6x/6	39x/1	20+/13	78-/41	61-/24	6x/6	12x/10	20x/6	15x/8	99+/13	160-/44	59x/2	20x/6	15x/8	99+/13	6x/6	39x/1	20+/13	78-/41	61-/24	6x/6
12x/3	20x/2	15x/2	13+/23	61-/24	12x/3	95+/6	4x/30	15+/102	131-/30	86+/27	75+/44	4x/30	15+/102	131-/30	12x/3	20x/2	15x/2	13+/23	61-/24	12x/3

1+5	9-8	4x4	16-3	5x3	19-2	9x2	1+5	9-8	4x4	16-3	5x3	19-2	9x2
16-3	5x3	19-2	9x2	32x2	50+12	79-6	30x2	50+6	6x9	9x2	46-29	23-7	16-3
9x2	46-29	70x10	9x8	14x10	139+2	20x7	25x5	14x10	139+1	25+27	20x3	9-8	4x4
23-7	79x1	12x10	76+9	89+30	76+9	29x5	16x10	99-6	22x4	20x7	29x5	50+12	46-29
9x2	30x2	78+2	94-7	16x10	25x6	99-6	160x1	29x5	94-7	76+9	70x10	9x8	17-3
16-3	50+6	23+7	32x2	50+12	29x5	120-1	50x2	29x3	32x2	50+12	23+7	32x2	4x4
4x4	6x9	8x4	29-8	46-9	79x1	32x2	50+12	79-6	160x1	12x10	2x22	70x10	9-8
46-29	25+27	7+22	5x5	20x2	99-6	8x4	29-8	46-9	22x4	7+22	8x6	50+12	5x3
1+5	20x3	29-8	46-9	16-3	7+36	23+7	5x5	20x2	89+30	30x2	7+36	78+2	46-29
16-3	17-3	2x22	7+22	4x4	46-29	8x4	46-9	20x2	29-8	50+6	9x8	16-3	17-3
9x2	4x4	8x6	8x4	29-8	1+5	7+22	9x3	8x4	120-1	6x9	32x2	9x2	4x4
23-7	46-29	7+36	7+22	5x5	20x2	29-8	34-7	7+22	29-8	25+27	70x10	23-7	46-29
9x2	1+5	16-3	50+6	4x6	23+7	9x3	8x4	29-8	46-9	50+12	17-3	9x2	1+5
16-3	19-2	9x2	25+27	20x3	30+2	34-7	7+22	5x5	20x2	78+2	4x4	16-3	19-2
4x4	23-7	23-7	46-29	32x2	50+12	79-6	70x10	9x8	79x1	19-2	46-29	4x4	23-7
46-29	9-8	9x2	1+5	23-7	9-8	4x4	16-3	5x3	19-2	9x2	1+5	46-29	9-8

1-20 White

21-40 Light grey

41-60 Grey

61-80 Dark grey

81-100 Orange

101-120 Pink

121-140 Light orange

141-160 Yellow

1+5	9-8	4x4	16-3	5x3	19-2	9x2	1+5	9-8	4x4	16-3	5x3	19-2	9x2	1+5
16-3	5x3	19-2	9x2	9-8	25+27	20x3	30x2	50+6	6x9	9x2	46-29	23-7	16-3	16-3
9x2	46-29	1+5	46-29	20x3	5x5	20x2	29-8	34-7	7+22	30x2	76+9	32x2	4x4	9x2
16-3	5x3	19-2	9x2	1+5	30x2	50+6	6x9	25+27	23+7	9x3	70x10	99-6	16-3	5x3
9x2	46-29	23-7	16-3	16-3	9-8	4x4	16-3	5x3	9x8	29-8	34-7	50+6	9x2	9-8
16-3	5x3	19-2	9x2	1+5	5x3	19-2	9x2	32x2	76+9	70x10	4x6	20x2	30x2	9x2
9x2	46-29	1+5	5x3	16-3	46-29	1+5	70x10	22x4	78+2	9-8	2x22	8x4	50+6	16-3
16-3	5x3	19-2	9x2	46-29	5x3	50+12	99-6	9x8	1+5	9x2	8x6	7+22	6x9	4x4
9x2	46-29	23-7	16-3	5x3	78+2	29x3	32x2	9-8	46-29	19-2	7+36	29-8	25+27	46-29
16-3	17-3	1+5	19-2	9x8	22x4	70x10	9x2	5x3	23-7	9x2	30x2	5x5	20x3	17-3
9x2	4x4	16-3	32x2	94-7	50+12	4x4	16-3	5x3	19-2	23-7	4x4	6x9	9-8	4x4
23-7	46-29	70x10	50x2	9x8	9x2	23-7	9x2	46-29	23-7	16-3	16-3	9-8	46-29	9-8
9x2	50+12	99-6	32x2	1+5	9-8	4x4	16-3	5x3	19-2	9x2	1+5	5x3	1+5	5x3
16-3	94-7	70x10	9x2	16-3	5x3	19-2	9x2	46-29	1+5	46-29	16-3	46-29	19-2	46-29
4x4	23-7	23-7	46-29	9x2	46-29	1+5	16-3	5x3	19-2	17-3	9x2	5x3	23-7	17-3
46-29	9-8	9x2	1+5	46-29	9-8	9x2	1+5	23-7	9-8	4x4	16-3	5x3	19-2	9x2

1-20 White   61-80 Brown
21-40 Blue   81-100 Dark Brown
41-60 Navy

1+5	5x3	1+5	5x3	9-8	4x4	16-3	5x3	19-2	9x2	1+5	5x3	1+5	5x3
16-3	46-29	19-2	46-29	5x3	19-2	9x2	46-29	1+5	46-29	16-3	46-29	19-2	46-29
23-7	9x2	20x2	29-8	34-7	7+22	29-8	20x2	29-8	34-7	7+22	29-8	23-7	9x2
9x2	46-29	23+7	9x3	8x4	29-8	46-9	23+7	9x3	8x4	29-8	46-9	9x2	46-29
16-3	9-8	30+2	34-7	7+22	5x5	20x2	30+2	34-7	7+22	5x5	20x2	16-3	9-8
23-7	16-3	20x2	29-8	34-7	7+22	29-8	20x2	29-8	34-7	7+22	29-8	23-7	16-3
46-29	9-8	34-7	119-8	16-3	29-8	46-9	23+7	9x3	9-8	49x2	34-7	46-29	9-8
23-7	9x2	20x2	29-8	34-7	30x2	50+6	6x9	25+27	34-7	7+22	29-8	23-7	9x2
9x2	46-29	23+7	9x3	8x4	79-6	46-9	23+7	70x10	8x4	29-8	46-9	9x2	46-29
16-3	9-8	30+2	34-7	7+22	20x3	30x2	50+6	6x9	7+22	5x5	20x2	16-3	9-8
23-7	16-3	20x2	29-8	34-7	8x4	29-8	46-9	23+7	34-7	7+22	29-8	23-7	16-3
46-29	9-8	23+7	9x3	8x4	29-8	46-9	23+7	9x3	8x4	29-8	46-9	46-29	9-8
1+5	5x3	1+5	5x3	9-8	4x4	16-3	5x3	19-2	9x2	1+5	5x3	1+5	5x3
16-3	46-29	19-2	46-29	5x3	19-2	9x2	46-29	1+5	46-29	16-3	46-29	19-2	46-29
9x2	5x3	23-7	17-3	46-29	1+5	16-3	5x3	19-2	17-3	9x2	5x3	23-7	17-3
16-3	5x3	19-2	9x2	9-8	9x2	1+5	23-7	9-8	4x4	16-3	5x3	19-2	9x2

1-20 White   41-60 Pink   81-100 Black

21-40 Light pink   61-80 Red

1+5	5x3	1+5	5x3	9-8	4x4	16-3	5x3	19-2	9x2	1+5	5x3	1+5	5x3	9x2	46-29
16-3	46-29	19-2	46-29	5x3	19-2	30x2	50+6	6x9	30x2	16-3	46-29	19-2	46-29	16-3	5x3
9x2	5x3	23-7	17-3	50+6	6x9	30+2	34-7	20x2	29-8	50+6	6x9	23-7	17-3	1+5	23-7
16-3	5x3	25+27	20x3	34-7	7+22	29-8	20x2	29-8	34-7	7+22	29-8	25+27	20x3	1+5	46-29
30x2	50+6	23+7	9x3	8x4	29-8	46-9	23+7	9x3	8x4	29-8	46-9	7+22	29-8	50+6	30x2
50+6	9x8	50+6	6x9	7+22	5x5	20x2	30+2	34-7	7+22	5x5	20x2	25+27	20x3	50+12	50+6
6x9	32x2	50+12	9x8	30x2	50+6	29-8	20x2	29-8	34-7	30x2	50+6	50+12	79x1	32x2	6x9
25+27	70x10	78+2	32x2	50+12	94-7	25+27	20x3	30x2	6x9	78+2	9x8	32x2	50+12	76+9	25+27
20x3	32x2	50+12	79-6	70x10	9x8	79x1	50+12	50+6	32x2	94-7	79-6	70x10	9x8	79x1	20x3
2x22	9x8	78+2	9x8	32x2	50+12	9x8	32x2	6x9	9x8	78+2	9x8	32x2	50+12	9x8	2x22
8x6	70x10	76+9	32x2	70x10	78+2	32x2	99-6	25+27	50+12	79-6	32x2	50+12	79-6	32x2	8x6
7+36	32x2	50+12	79-6	32x2	50+12	79-6	32x2	20x3	32x2	50+12	29x3	70x10	9x8	79x1	7+36
50+6	79-6	32x2	50+12	79-6	70x10	9x8	79x1	2x22	9x8	78+2	9x8	32x2	50+12	9x8	50+6
25+27	50+6	9x8	78+2	9x8	32x2	50+12	9x8	8x6	32x2	50+12	79-6	9x8	78+2	50+6	25+27
5x3	19-2	30x2	50+6	70x10	78+2	50x2	50+12	7+36	9x8	78+2	9x8	50+6	6x9	5x3	19-2
9x2	5x3	46-29	1+5	25+27	20x3	9x8	32x2	50+6	79-6	25+27	20x3	19-2	17-3	9x2	5x3
16-3	9x2	9-8	9x2	4x4	16-3	50+6	6x9	25+27	30x2	19-2	9x2	9-8	4x4	16-3	9x2

1-20 White   41-60 Black   81-100 Gray
21-40 Green   61-80 Brown

1+5	9-8	4x4	16-3	1+5	9-8	9x2	46-29	5x3	9-8	1+5	9-8	4x4	16-3	1+5
16-3	5x3	19-2	9x2	16-3	5x3	16-3	5x3	9x8	79x1	16-3	5x3	19-2	9x2	16-3
9x2	46-29	1+5	46-29	9x2	46-29	5x3	32x2	8x4	9x8	9x2	46-29	1+5	46-29	9x2
16-3	5x3	19-2	9x2	16-3	5x3	50+12	34-7	7+22	32x2	16-3	5x3	19-2	9x2	16-3
9x2	46-29	23-7	16-3	9x2	78+2	29-8	8x4	29-8	46-9	70x10	79-6	23-7	16-3	9x2
16-3	5x3	19-2	9x2	32x2	7+22	5x5	7+22	5x5	79-6	30x2	50+12	19-2	9x2	5x3
9x2	46-29	1+5	5x3	79-6	70x10	9x8	20x2	32x2	50+6	79-6	34-7	32x2	50+12	79-6
16-3	5x3	19-2	9x2	16-3	1+5	9x2	70x10	6x9	9x8	29-8	20x2	29-8	34-7	70x10
9x2	46-29	23-7	16-3	9x2	16-3	79-6	25+27	32x2	7+22	46-9	23+7	9x3	79-6	46-29
16-3	17-3	1+5	19-2	46-29	9x8	20x3	9x8	9x2	9x8	20x2	30+2	9x8	46-29	5x3
9x2	46-29	23-7	16-3	79-6	2x22	70x10	19-2	46-29	50+12	29-8	32x2	16-3	5x3	19-2
16-3	5x3	19-2	9x8	7+36	79-6	5x3	23-7	17-3	78+2	9x8	5x3	9-8	4x4	16-3
5x3	1+5	32x2	8x6	9x8	16-3	5x3	19-2	9x2	16-3	46-29	4x4	16-3	19-2	9x2
46-29	9x8	50+6	32x2	5x3	9-8	4x4	16-3	5x3	19-2	9x2	1+5	5x3	1+5	5x3
32x2	25+27	9x8	19-2	46-29	5x3	19-2	9x2	46-29	1+5	46-29	16-3	46-29	19-2	46-29
79-6	70x10	5x3	23-7	17-3	46-29	1+5	16-3	5x3	19-2	17-3	9x2	5x3	23-7	17-3
9x2	16-3	5x3	19-2	9x2	9-8	9x2	1+5	23-7	9-8	4x4	16-3	5x3	19-2	9x2

1-20 White   41-60 Brown
21-40 Grey   61-80 Black

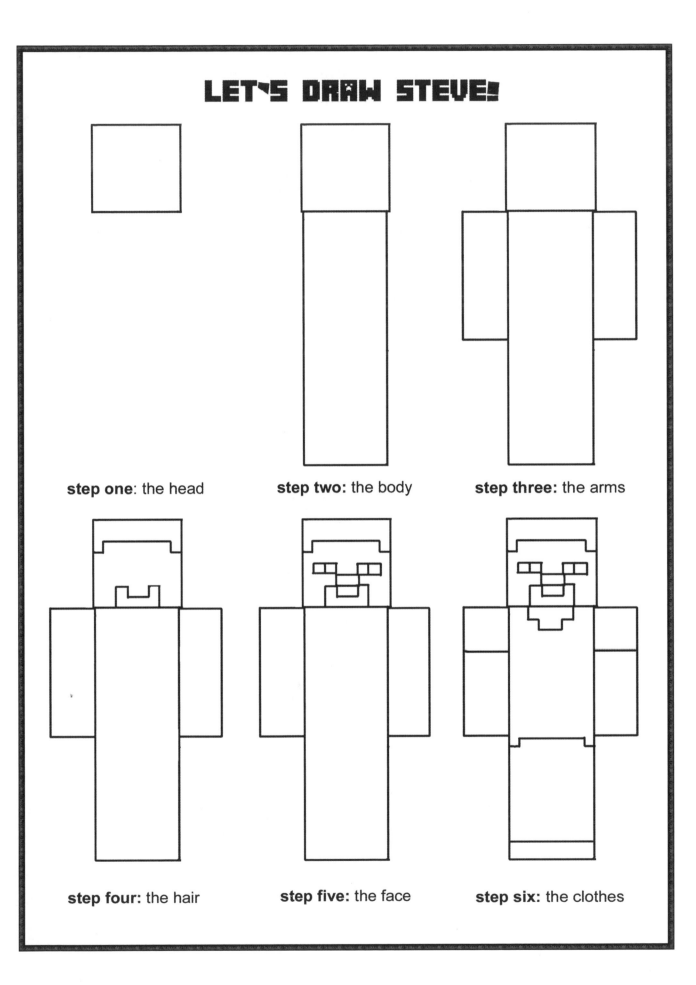

LET'S DRAW STEVE!

step one: the head

step two: the body

step three: the arms

step four: the hair

step five: the face

step six: the clothes

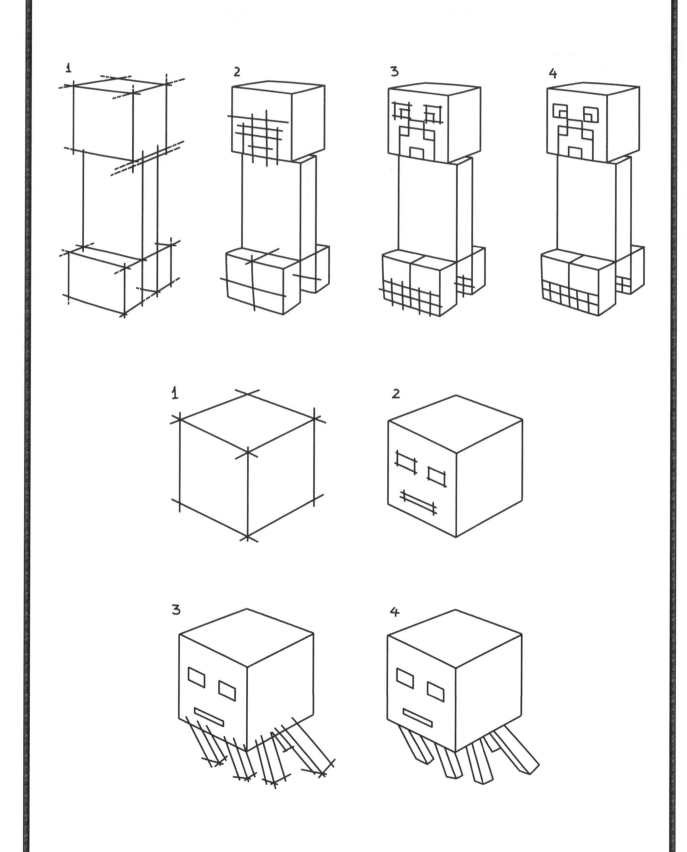

LET'S DRAW A CREEPER!

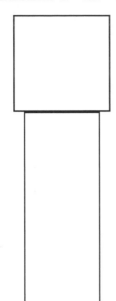

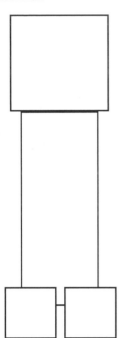

step one: the head

step two: the body

step three: the legs

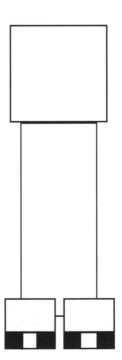

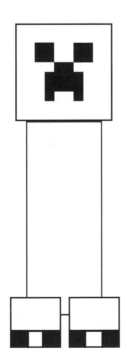

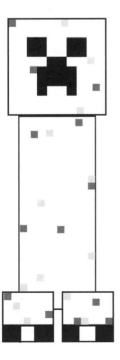

step four: the feet

step five: the face

step six: pixel colors

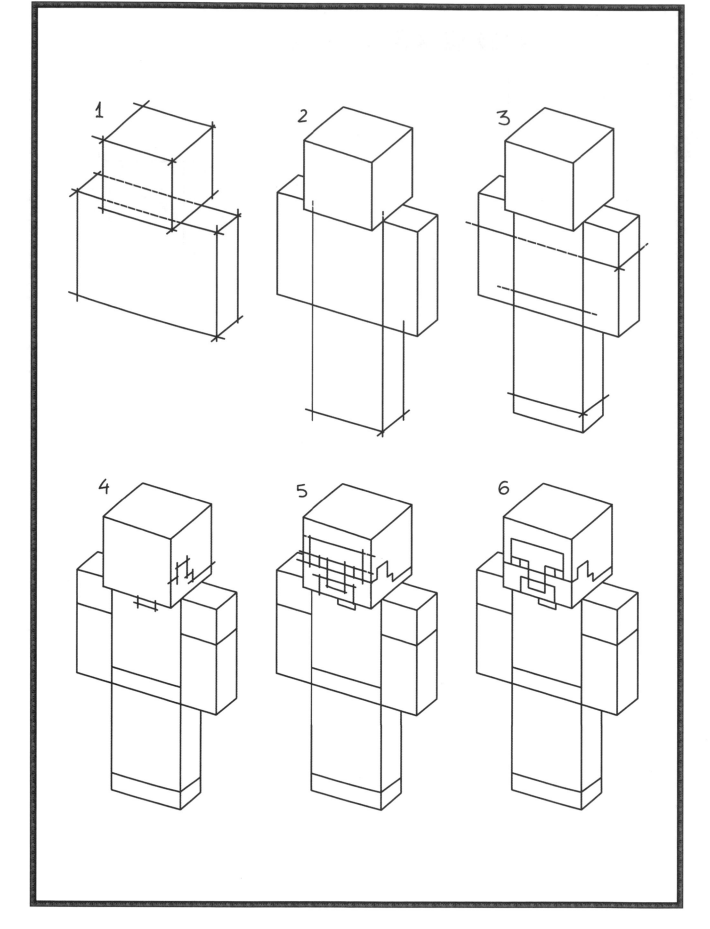

LET'S DRAW ENDERMAN!

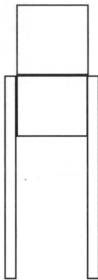

step one: the head

step two: the body

step three: the arms

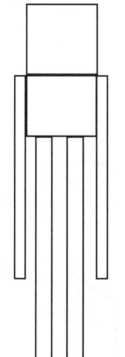

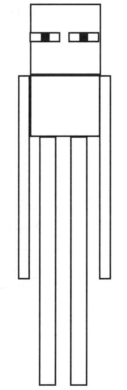

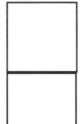

step four: the legs

step five: the eyes

step six: color

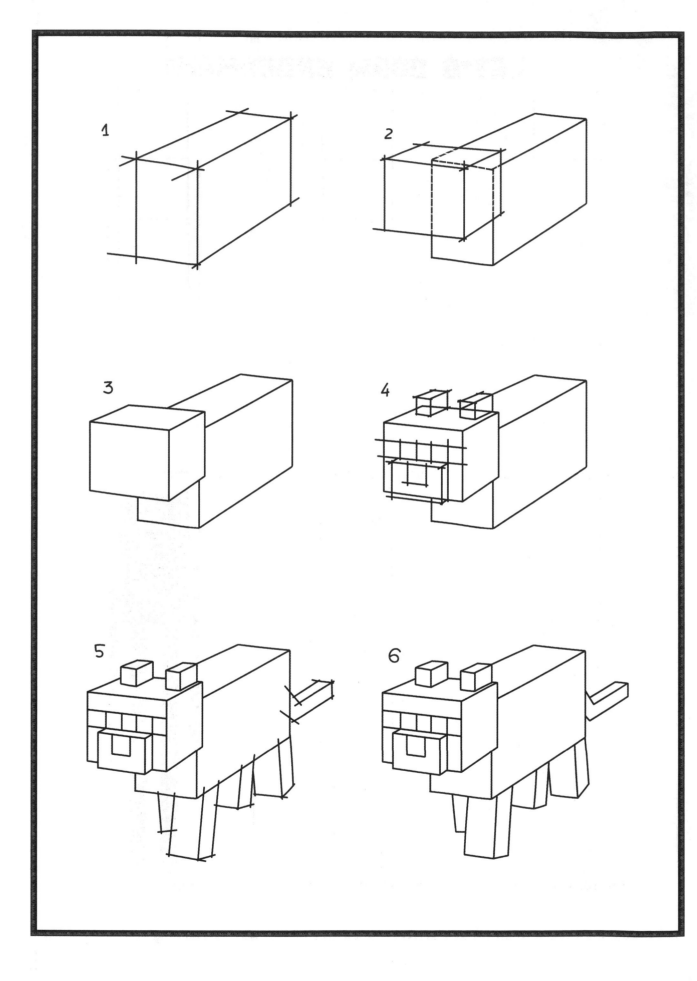

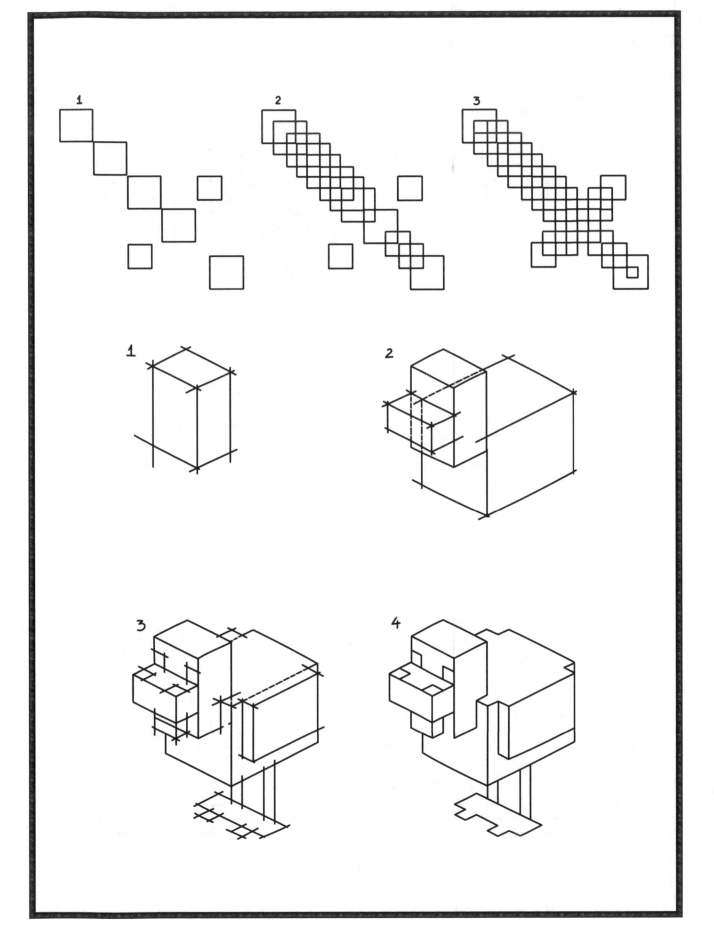

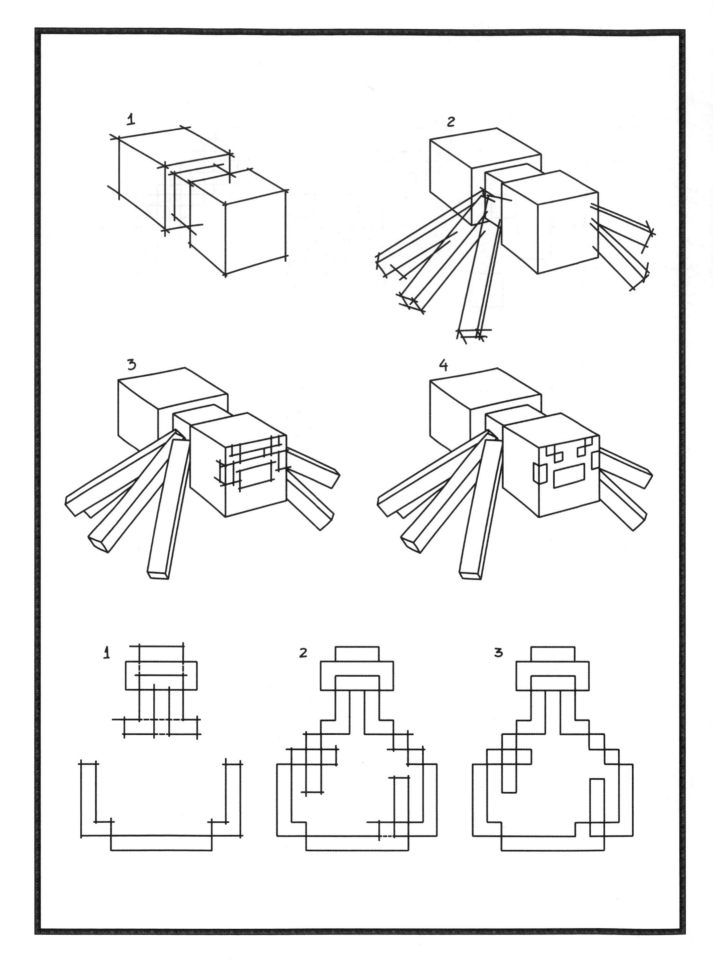

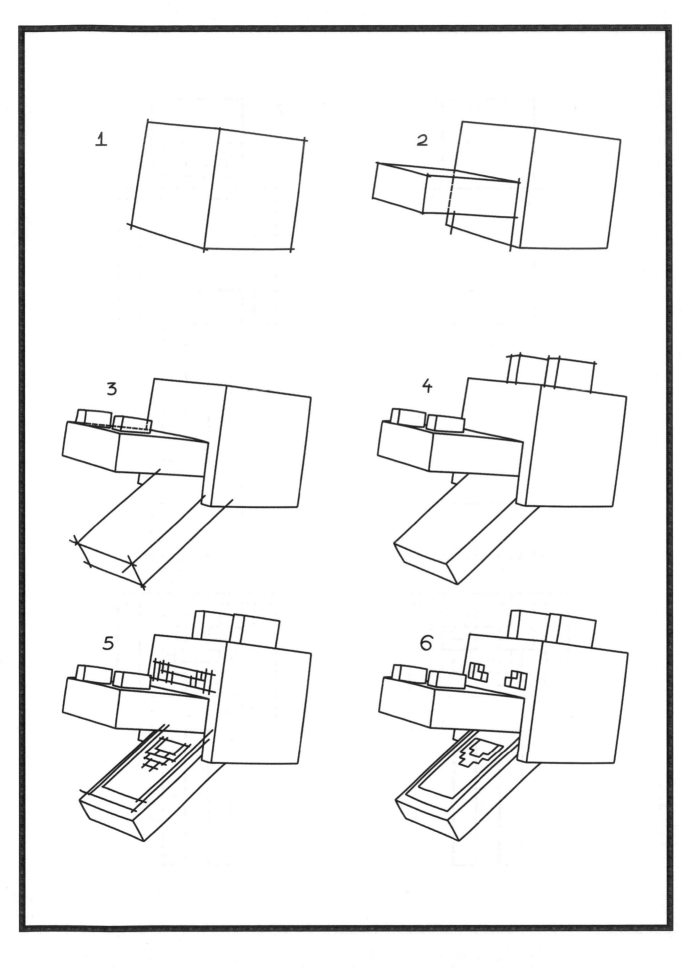

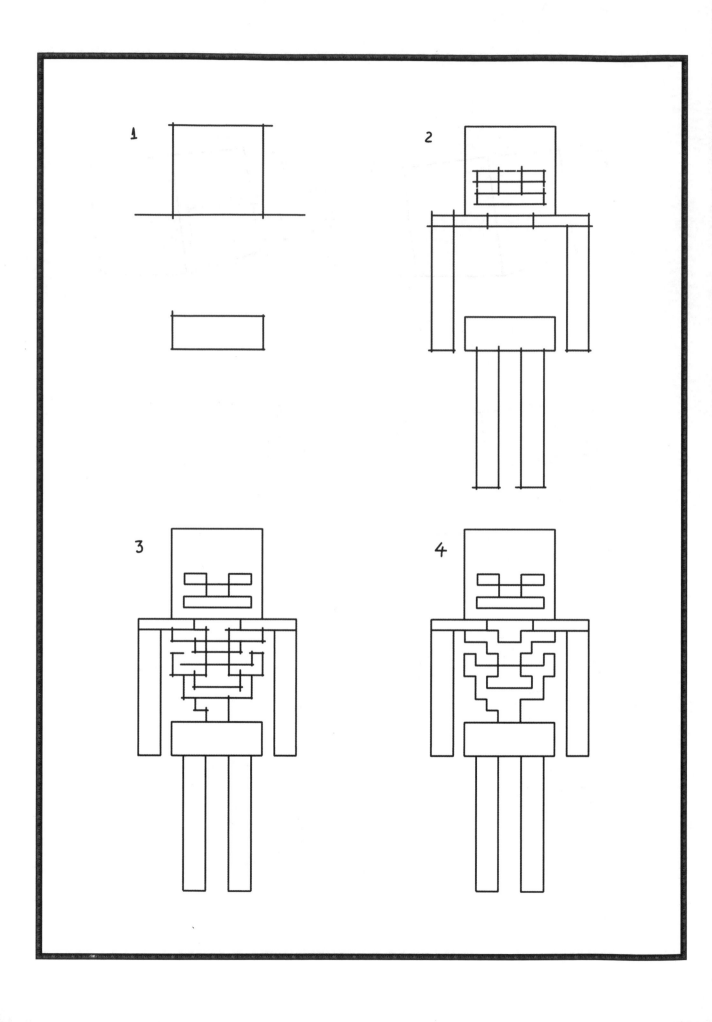

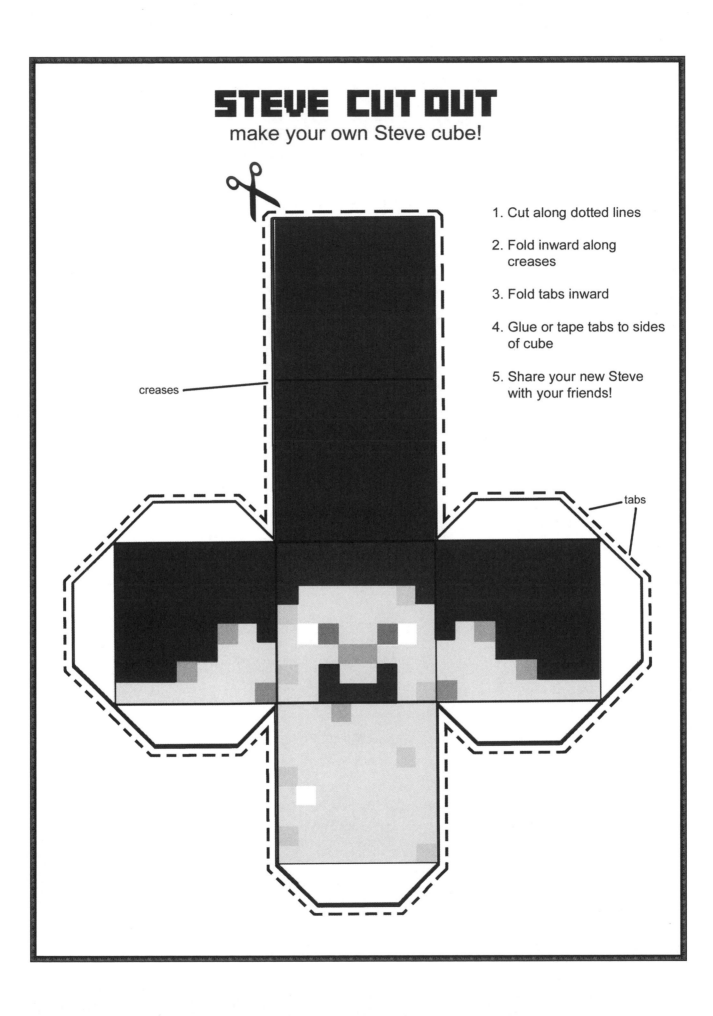

STEVE CUT OUT
make your own Steve cube!

creases

tabs

1. Cut along dotted lines

2. Fold inward along creases

3. Fold tabs inward

4. Glue or tape tabs to sides of cube

5. Share your new Steve with your friends!

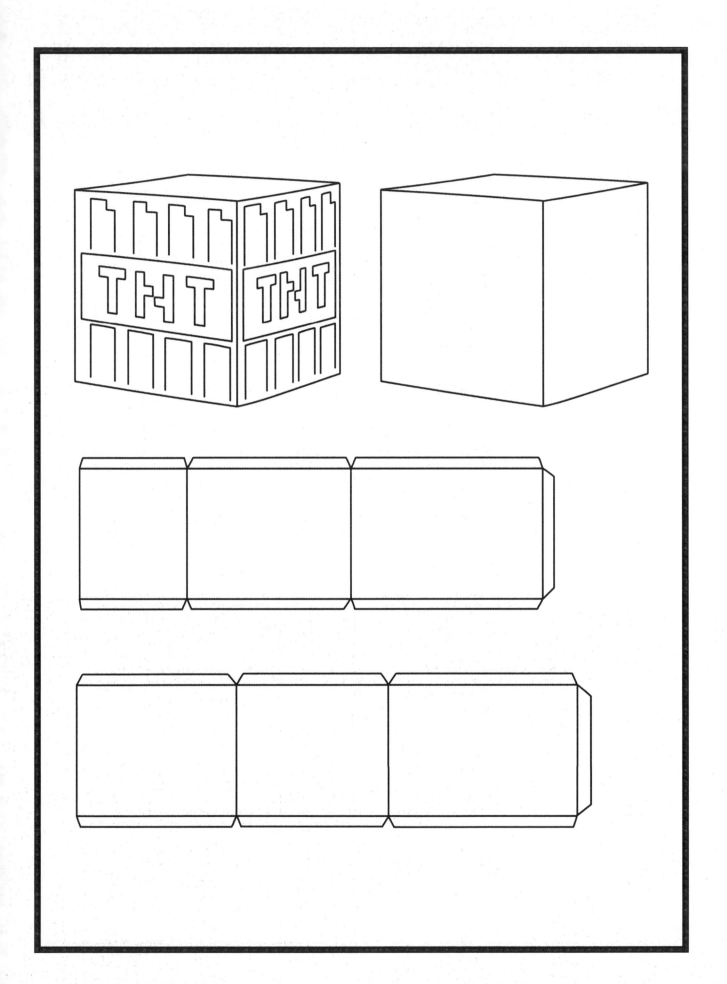

CREEPER CUT OUT
make your own Creeper cube!

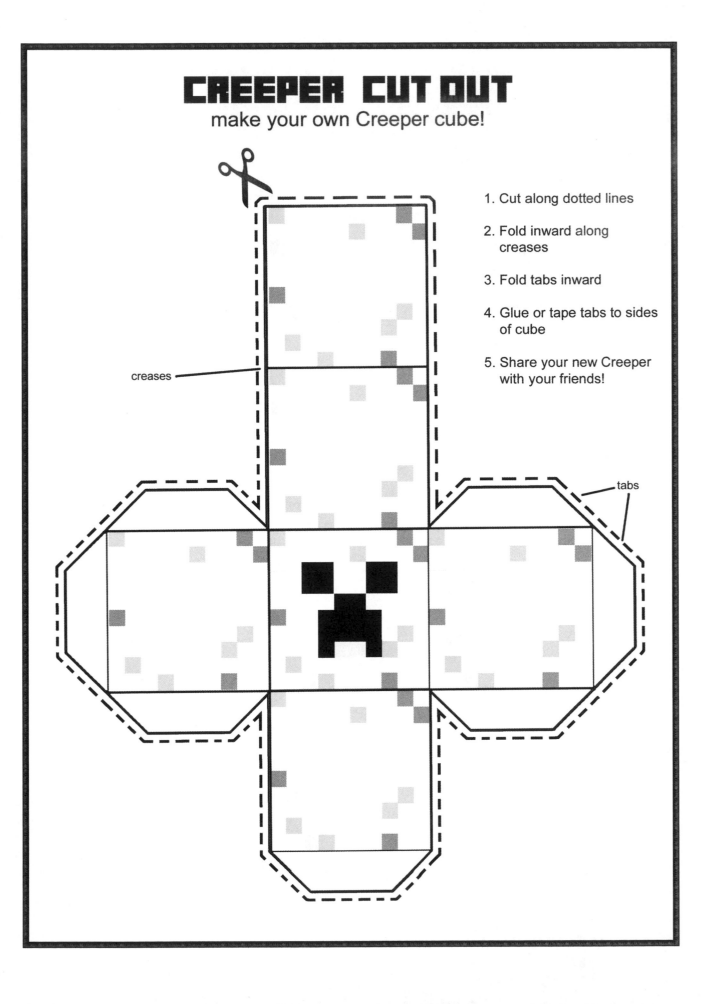

1. Cut along dotted lines

2. Fold inward along creases

3. Fold tabs inward

4. Glue or tape tabs to sides of cube

5. Share your new Creeper with your friends!

creases

tabs

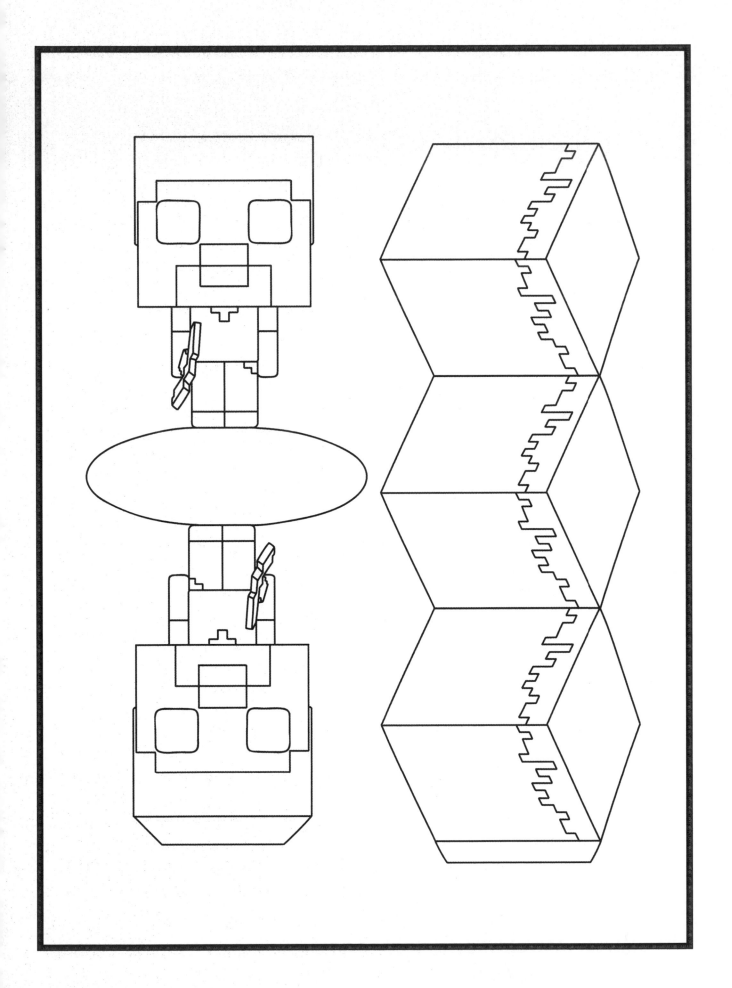

WOLF CUT OUT
make your own Wolf cube!

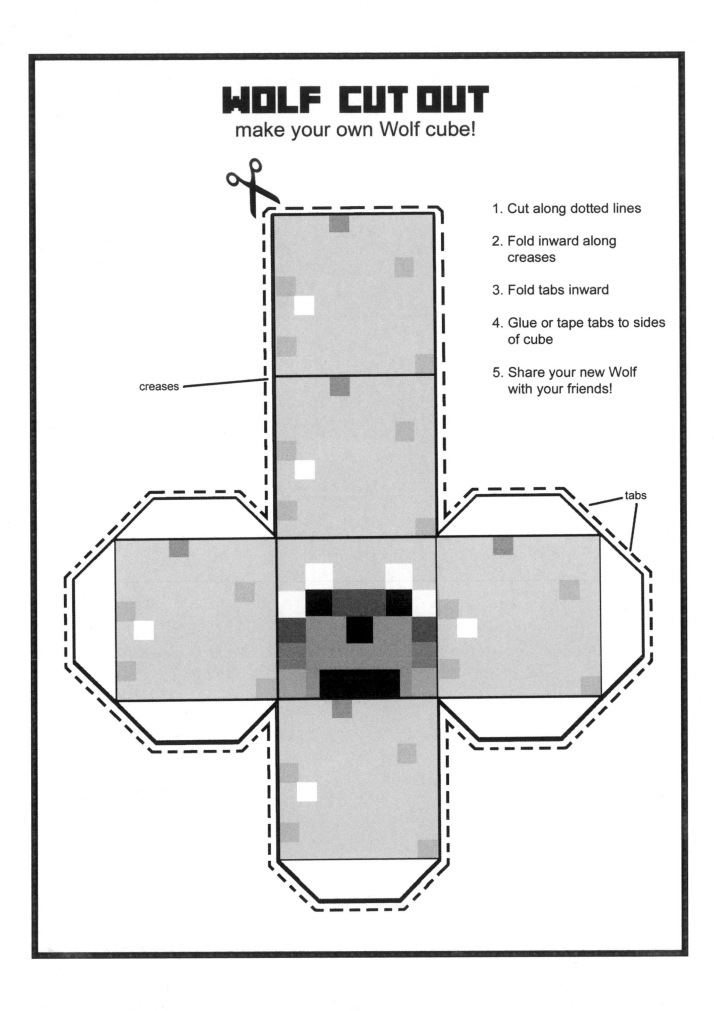

1. Cut along dotted lines

2. Fold inward along creases

3. Fold tabs inward

4. Glue or tape tabs to sides of cube

5. Share your new Wolf with your friends!

creases

tabs

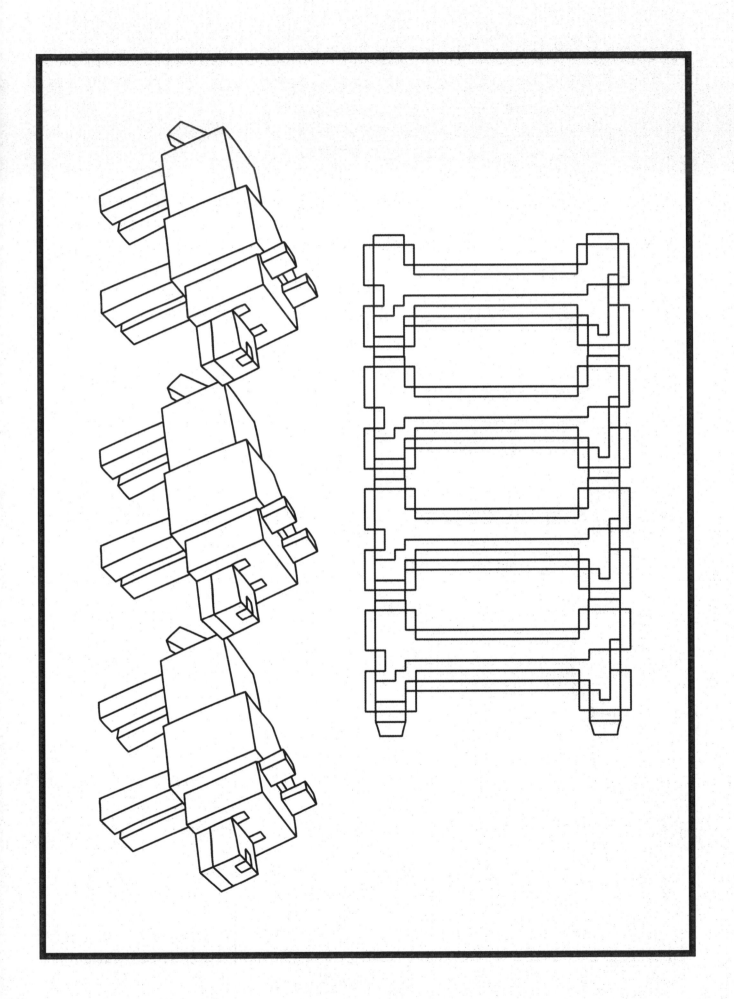

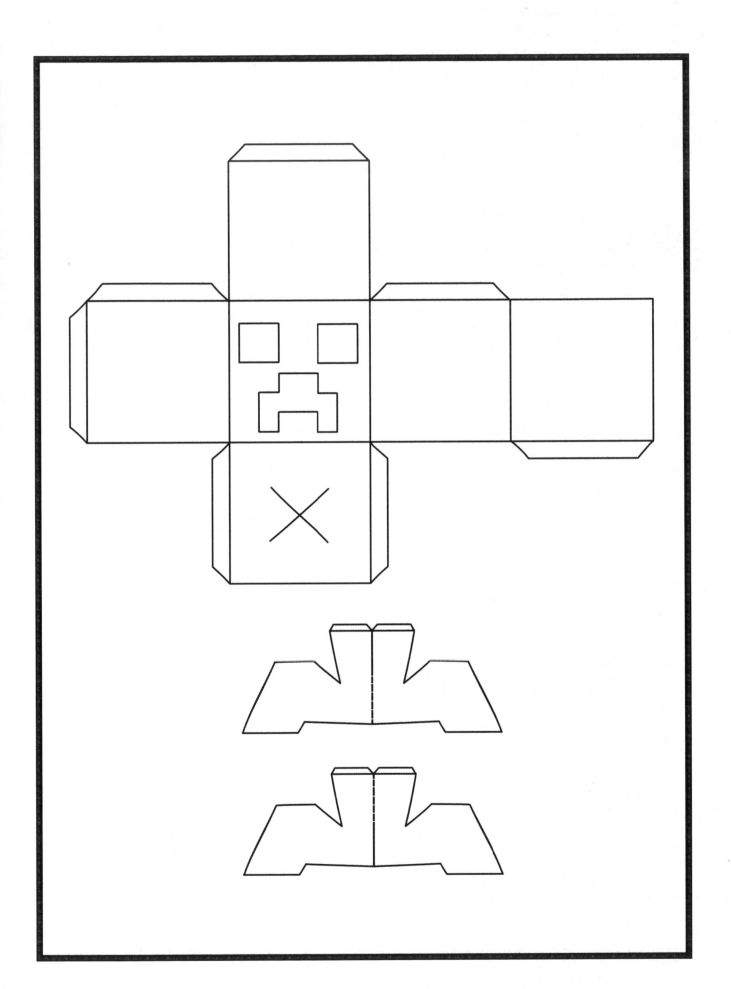

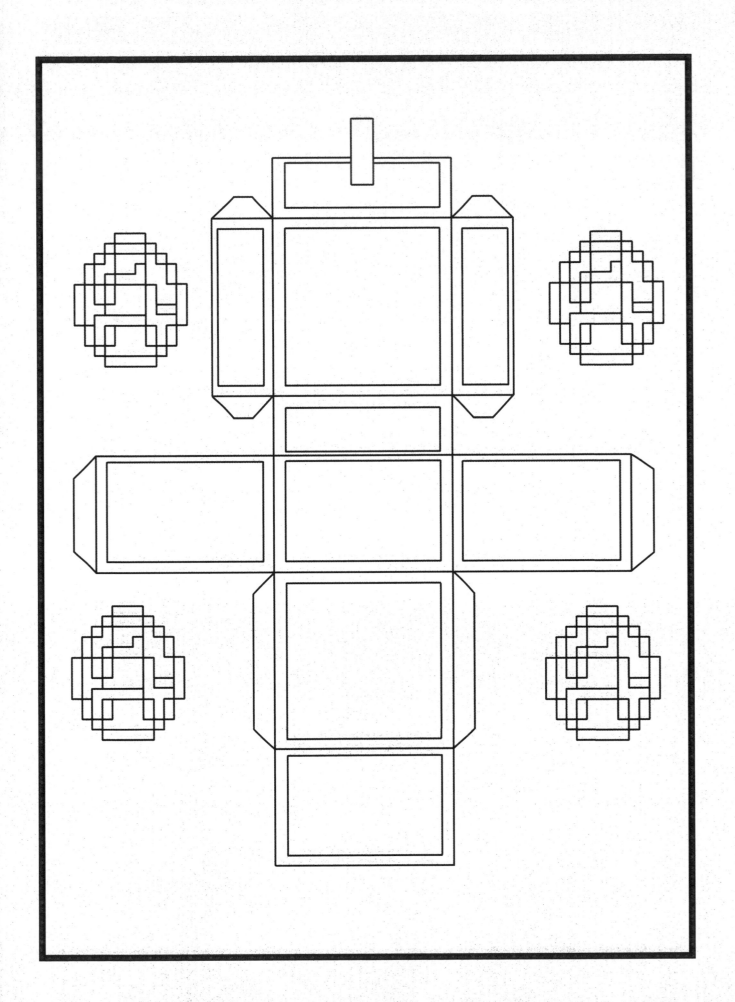

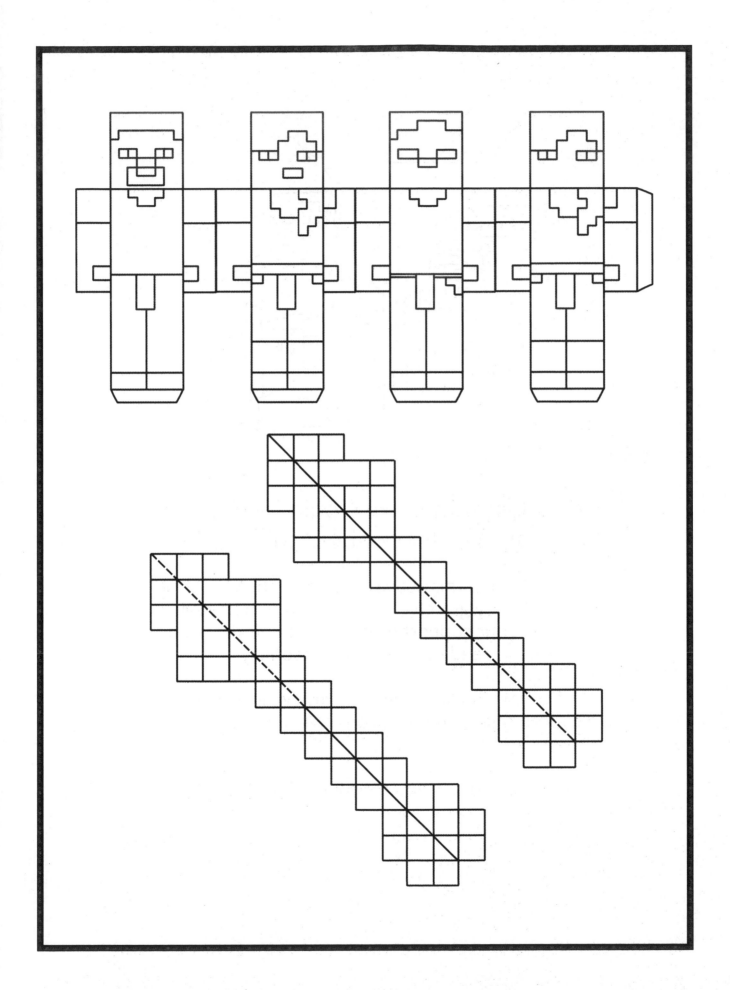

One last thing - we would love to hear your feedback about this book!

If you found this activity book fun and useful, we would be very grateful if you posted a short review on Amazon! Your support does make a difference and we read every review personally.

If you would like to leave a review, just head on over to this book's Amazon page and click "Write a customer review".

Thank you for your support!